## Praise

"Eddie Dobbins makes a profoundly inspirational debut with *Tea with Mom*. With eloquence and compassion, this son shares the experience of being his mother's caregiver before cancer ended her life. While his story is personal, the lessons are universal, and a timely contribution for the many caregivers who are walking the same path today. This is a beautiful gift."

—REV. IYANLA VANZANT, host of "Iyanla: Fix My Life" and author of *Get Over It: Thought Therapy for Healing the Hard Stuff*

"*Tea with Mom* begins where *Eat Pray Love* ends. A journey of grieving on the Island of Bali, Indonesia, this is a memoir of profound healing, forgiveness and self-love."

—CHIP CONLEY, author of *Wisdom@Work: The Making of a Modern Elder* and founder of Joie de Vivre Hotels

"*Tea with Mom* is a journey into the soul of authentic, hard-won forgiveness. At the same time, it is a celebration of life; of poetry, music, cafes, foods and scents. Dobbins somehow holds love, redemption, abuse and God all together, with poetic, lush wisdom. It's a piece of art—and I encourage you not to miss it!"

—KEN PAGE, LCSW, author of *Deeper Dating: How to Drop the Games of Seduction and Discover the Power of Intimacy*

"*Tea with Mom* is a beautifully written, courageous book for those on a spiritual path, for those dealing with grief, and for all lovers of great writing. Eddie captures the beauty, sensuality and spirituality of Bali as he seeks healing for his grief. His book is an eloquent, profound and beautifully written exploration of one man's spiritual journey."

—DIANA GREENTREE, actress and author of
*The Camros Bird*

"In *Tea with Mom*, Eddie Dobbins takes us on a spiritual adventure that embraces his own divinity and the spiritual principles of loving, compassion and self-forgiveness. After having cared for his mother at the end of her journey of life, Eddie shares his own journey of healing filled with wisdom, exploration and self-reflection. The eloquence and poetry in his words touch to the deepest part of one's being, speaking to the sacredness found in the spiritual lessons of life. *Tea with Mom* will serve as an inspiration to many as they witness through Eddie's words the beauty inherent in all of life's experiences."

—DRS. RON AND MARY HULNICK, marriage and
family therapists, and co-authors of *Loyalty to Your Soul:
The Heart of Spiritual Psychology*

# Tea *with* Mom

## Spiritual Lessons on Life and Death, and Healing in Bali

A CAREGIVER'S MEMOIR

*Athumi!*
*Let, Love, Read!*
*Eddie*

# Eddie L. Dobbins, Jr., M.A.

Jupiter, Wheatley & Wells Publishing
Mill Valley, California

ISBN 978-1-7328914-0-1  (print)
ISBN 978-1-7328914-1-8  (ebook)

Library of Congress Control Number: 2018913099

Book design by Val Sherer
Cover design by Doug Baird Productions
Front cover photo copyright Eddie L. Dobbins, Jr.
Back cover photo copyright Suki Zoe

Published by Jupiter, Wheatley & Wells Publishing
www.jupiterwheatleyandwellspublishing.com

For information, contact the author at:
www.eddiedobbins.com

Printed in the United States of America

To Rita Barbara Rosch,
who showed me grace in the midst of darkness,
and
to 1.3 million youth caregivers nationwide.

# Contents

# Foreword

Eddie's moving book about compassion, healing and care-giving takes his readers on a journey of self-reflection and life lessons he learned while taking care of his mother for 203 days before her death.

Each word, a poet's voice, a dance, a rhythm of delight, moved me when Eddie shared his touching story with me at my home in San Francisco in 2017. Death is something we cannot avoid, and his loving tribute to his mother is also an exploration of Eddie's personal story—his courage, strength and humor as he moved through one of the most difficult journeys of his life.

If you are taking care of a parent or sibling, or embracing a "life or death" experience, I'd like to share with you what I told Eddie years ago as Mayor of San Francisco: "You will beat this."

—Mayor Willie L. Brown, Jr., San Francisco, California

# CHAPTER 1

# I See Clearly with the Light from Within

## Ubud, Bali, Indonesia – December 6, 2011

*You've experienced what healers call the Christ Plane; you crossed over and gained access to the other side.* Words float through compressed air, to the pen, to paper. Feathers from an invisible sky of light blues, turquoise, hues of grey nudge against puffed clouds outside the oval-eye window of my plane. Interwoven words, alphabets floating, hovering in space. Words of a guide, a teacher who opened a window and showed me how to fly into the unknown, into a place I now recognize as home. Words that connect me to a moving stream of consciousness grounded in love and divine intuition.

In the past, the unknown was fear in a stream of consciousness grounded in judgment. It traveled from my feet, up my legs, through my intestines, to my throat, and radiated out of the crown of my shaved head. My third eye was blocked, blinded. I hurt. A pain cloaked in tears, masked, wrapped, waiting and watching for guidance, for signs that would lead me on my journey toward healing. *Will it happen in Bali?*

I intend to acknowledge the gifts that unfold from the Island of the Gods as I embark, in gratitude, on a solo journey. I will allow Spirit to use me in service to others, as I am in service to myself.

I desire to elope with myself into the loving embrace of the island's magic and spirit. I will mourn, knowing I did the best with what I had, as my mother's caregiver for 203 days. I intend to rest.

I plan to nurture my body with vibrant organic foods. I intend to uncover, probe and honor the lingering questions I have about death, and life with my mother.

I will honor what comes forward as I move through my grief.

I intend to synthesize all my resources for creative expression and rejoice in interconnectedness through my heart. I intend to balance my openness to the Universe and the hidden magic on the island.

I will hold my mission, vision and dreams close to my heart regardless of the turbulence I am experiencing as the plane dips on this flight from Singapore to Bali. I send loving energy to the pilot, the co-pilot and the autopilot system.

I intend to move through the bumps, dips, jolts of grief and memories that appear in the moment. I intend to shape this journey for the highest good of all concerned.

I am guided by Spirit as I remove obstacles that might

impede the natural course of my grieving.

I will release the knots in my body and mind through touch and the flow of ancient aromatic oils, detoxifying salts and herbs. I will revel in the lush river valley setting, allowing its beauty to flush away the tension nipping at my muscles.

I intend to acknowledge *life*.

✎

*She is dead.* The words echo in harmony in my head as I listen to the plucked strings, xylophones, barrel instruments and bamboo flutes playing "Long Journey" from a Balinese Buddha Bar CD mix. The melodies murmur from the rear speakers in the corner of the Art Kaffee on Jalan Monkey Forest *(Jalan* indicates a road). I attempt to integrate the cacophony of sounds from within and without, while alternately journaling and savoring a selection of Indonesian curries mixed with exotic spices—sour to sweet and hot, lemongrass and chilies.

I also indulge in people-watching, noticing a twinge of jet lag and weariness move through my body. My limbs dangle in the hot stickiness. Flies nip and buzz, swoosh and cling to the sweat dribbling down my skin.

The Art Kaffee is squeezed between narrow dirt and patched concrete alleyways that allow only enough room for individual scooters, small buggies or bicycles to pass.

The Kaffee's quirky bamboo hut was my go-to place for healthy food during my first visit to Bali in 2009. The food is still as good as it was then. The fusion cuisine combines Mexican, Javanese and a touch of Thai. It pops on my palate, penetrating serenity.

The Kaffee's furnishings and art and aromas create an atmosphere as welcoming as a friend's home—a warm take-off-your-shoes, breathe-and-unwind ambiance. It is so unlike my mother's home, where I spent most of the last year.

Odd-shaped mirrors, simply hung, deflect unwanted energy and create a feng shui flow. The Kaffee's narrow space is scented by candles in small glass containers on each table. Though I feel invisible in my silent grief, I joyfully embrace the beeps and bellows of the late afternoon traffic as vehicles careen through and around the potholes of Jalan Monkey Forest.

Solitude is calling my name, though I am surrounded by other tourists, who like me, are on a "Long Journey," resting, journaling and absorbing their new surroundings with all senses alert. Bali demands attention from the senses: The profusion of colorful fabrics draped over bannisters and hanging from balconies, the baskets of bright fruits adorning the stalls of outdoor markets. The mix of traffic fumes with fragrant blossoms and the collective odor of humanness. The soft cotton batik sarong wrapped around my waist. The pleasure of turmeric, basil, garlic concoctions, especially combined with ground chilies.

I keep my eyes hidden behind sunglasses, which cannot shield the cascading tears on my cheeks. Even so, I take in the Kaffee's holiday decorations.

Ornaments created out of Indonesian newspapers—stars, snowmen and Christmas trees—hang by thinly threaded laced bamboo all around the Kaffee. A five-foot-tall plastic pine tree sits on a cloth sprinkled with spray-can snow. Small wrapped boxes under the tree remind me of bleak Christmases in my past. The memory passes as I turn my attention to the Kaffee garden, where a mix of bambu tali and tropical flowers—Bird of Paradise, hibiscus, delicate Jepun—are dancing in the wind.

Mixed with the holiday décor are small Tibetan flags of blue, green and yellow on lengths of string crisscrossing the Kaffee, displaying a rainbow of Sanskrit words meaning hope and peace. The flags spin and flap and clap like leaves in the flow of dry air spewing from a white swivel fan listing in the corner.

Afternoon traffic continues to build. Mopeds buzz and bicycles zigzag through the maze of congestion. Vendors hawk pungent steaming soups of vegetables and fish. Stray dogs dart in and out of traffic, gobbling fallen scraps of food. Tourists weave in and out of the melee, avoiding the men positioned every one hundred feet holding up signs that say "TAXI."

The pungent smells of earth, river and tropical rainforest, the incessant traffic noise, the rush and flap of colors, the abundant holiday décor and the maze of people all combine to partially numb the memory of death that clings to me.

I write feverishly, as if my life depends on it. When I look up and see a mother and son walking side by side down Jalan Monkey Forest, I am jarred with emotion. A sharp chill moves through me like tingling neuropathy. Sorrow coils inside me, moving from feet to tailbone, touching my kidneys, rising up my back, nipping my neck. My throat constricts and my cheeks swell as I give way to tears.

"Long Journey" plays in my head as I sit with my journal open to a blank page. Questions leap from my pen, like tadpoles in the lily pond in the rear garden.

*Why?*

*Why, Eddie, did you give up your life as you knew it to return to Chicago?*

I write down everything that comes, transcribing my thoughts on the thin lines etched across the page. Perspiration slides from my head down my olive skin.

❦

Questions come at me like the darts I hear hitting the

board behind me.

*Why did I give up my career, friends and six-figure income, to return to Chicago in March 2011 to be my mother's caregiver?*

*Did I have something to prove to her?*

*Was my return to Chicago a last-ditch effort to obtain some degree of loving before her death?*

*Did she know what I was sacrificing?*

*Did she know I contributed to our living expenses by cashing out my retirement accounts?*

*Did she care?*

*Did she take me for granted during the days and nights I watched over her?*

*Did she love me?*

*Why didn't I give up, return to San Francisco and resume my former life?*

*Did she know that the photograph of me sleeping next to her would be our last picture together?*

*Did she know how much I loved her, that I would not have traded the experience of taking care of her to do anything else, to be anywhere else?*

*What was it that compelled me to radically change my life to be with my mother, a person I always believed did not understand, embrace or love me?*

I scrawl these questions across the paper.

*Why Ubud? Why halfway around the world?*

Ubud's draw for me is a deep question of inquiry. I am a black man in an Asian country. Am I returning to my ancestral roots?

∽

"Good afternoon, sir." A man's voice rustles from a few feet away.

I glance up at him, suspending my feverish writing for a moment. In one hand he holds a black plastic tray with an etched bamboo lining. His other hand rests on his backside, tucked between his jeans and underwear.

In the light of the Kaffee, our skin tones seem to entwine, and pixels of yellow, golden caramel and green flit against the shadowed interior. He crosses the planked bamboo floor to my table, walking with the delicate steps of an untrained dancer. He emanates a joyful and childlike innocence. His coarse black hair is cropped, jelled slick, perfectly trimmed.

"I will take the check, please," I say, from the same position I've been sitting in for close to six hours. He extends his hand. His scent is a small jolt of electricity, of remembering.

"Hello, brother," he says, a warm energetic beckoning of his hand, a shake, a sense of lost souls reconnecting. His charm and charisma command attention.

"Hello, Agung," I say, embarrassed, only now noticing

his name embroidered on his shirt, jarring my memory of our first meeting two years ago. He seemed a child then, a man now.

I have been anchored in deep reflection—ruminating on Ubud, the magic, the economic disparity between myself and the people of Bali, the poverty and hardship—conditions with which I am only vaguely familiar. Bali's paradise is set amongst steep ravines and pristine rice paddies, each paddy seeded by hand, a ceremony supported by the belief in the karmic value of cultivating harmony and tranquility through hard work. I am sitting in the epicenter of a culture radically different from that of the South Side of Chicago.

"How long have been here?" he asks, enunciating each word with equal weight and emphasis. "Here" becomes a two-syllable word with the stress on the second syllable, the first "e" sounding like the "a" in "May."

"I just arrived in Bali," I reply. "I've returned to recover from taking care of my mother while she was dying. I've come to heal myself, and to tune into the wisdom, vitality and peace I feel here on the island."

As I move my journal and belongings into my backpack, Agung speaks, a reflective sadness in his eyes. "You are just steps away from the Great Temple of Death."

At first his words sound like one big gurgle. All I hear is "death."

"In the sacred monkey forest … you should go there to pray." He pauses, noticing my interest.

"Why is it sacred?" I ask.

Blacky, the mixed lab with a patch of white on his forehead, rustles beneath the table, watching for falling scraps.

The Great Temple of Death, known as Pura Dalem Agung, dates back to the fourteenth century, but I do not know this yet.

"She is the goddess of death," he explains as he walks to the rear of the Kaffee to deposit the dishes from my table. Turning like Peter Falk in "Colombo," with the tray in one hand, he says with an upper-caste accent, "Brother …"

I look in his direction. The Isley Brothers' "Harvest for the World" is playing in the background.

"She symbols motherly love." He smiles at me gently.

Touched by Agung's departing words, I wave goodbye as the lyrics move through my head and through the Kaffee. The song of love and need and celebrating life pulls at me, and I lose myself in listening.

My phone buzzes in the pocket of my shorts, under my sarong.

"Where are you, boy?" the voice on the other end of the line asks.

"Dad! How are you?" I'm delighted to hear from him.

"How was your flight?" I head out of the Kaffee toward my Balinese compound on Jalan Sri Wedari.

"It was great."

His baritone chuckle vibrates through the phone. "I was thinking of the time you called me from Germany, collect. Too bad I can't do that to you now." We laugh.

"Dad! It's so beautiful here. I wish you could be with me. I know returning to Bali will be healing."

"Son, enjoy yourself. Rest, and remember to talk to the Lord if you need some guidance." I know he says this not as a suggestion but as direction.

"I will. I'll give you a call when I return to Chicago. Love you!"

"Love you too, son," he says with compassion, indicating he knows that the 203 days I spent caring for my mother were life-altering.

# CHAPTER 2

# I Synthesize All of My Resources for Focused Creative Expression

**Chicago, Illinois: Western Suburbs –**

**After Thanksgiving, 2011**

"A Traditional Balinese Compound!" The headline jumped from the screen: "Pick me, pick me!" I was scanning hundreds of listings in and around Ubud for my return. "Serenity. Sacred Traditions. Continuity. Family." The descriptions pulled my heartstrings, a yo-yo, suspended in fragile uncertainty. I was consumed by memories. I needed a break. A time-out.

❧

In the 1960's, just north of old U.S. Route 66, adjacent to Illinois Route 53, a modern village was born in the farm fields. It was a time in Illinois history known as "white flight," when whites scurried to the "western suburbs," spurred by segregation. My mother moved into this suburb in the 1980's and lived there until she died four weeks before Thanksgiving, inhabiting the eighteen-hundred-square-foot, three-bedroom, two-bath ranch house I became responsible for. I decided that packing, selling, storing, shipping, cleaning, painting, moving and renting could wait. I was eager to return home to San Francisco. But the when and the how plagued me, as did my mother's final words, "Make sure you have an alternative plan."

*How will I survive this? How will I survive?* I sat glued to the brown-speckled, cream-colored two-cushion couch parked against the mahogany veneer paneling. A ceramic clock hung above, peering out into the snow-covered yard visible through frosted glass patio doors. The cream vertical blinds were pulled to the side. I had been gazing at these surroundings from my stationary position for weeks, in solitude, in the dark—waiting, watching, waiting to jump back into life.

The depression had kicked in; the couch became my connection to my mother, to her heartbeat, to the invisible cord that connected us. Each room was cluttered with wall-to-wall furnishings, perfectly placed as she'd left them. *Where do I start? Where do I begin? How do I replenish? How do I maintain a forward motion in confidence and alignment?* Questions rose like uncontrollable tics.

❧

"Good evening, Mr. Dobbins. Thank you for calling United Airlines 1K. How may I help you?" The chipper voice made me feel like I was talking to one of Santa's helpers.

"I know it's the end of November, but by any chance are there any seats available to Denpasar for award miles?" I asked with fingers crossed. Sheets of snow pummeled the windows and the wind howled. I waited with phone to my ear, reclining on the couch, wrapped in a white blanket, immersed in my mother's scent. I was sipping fresh brewed tea from my mother's glass mug imprinted with maple leaf designs. Perhaps I was paying homage to her by drinking out of that mug, commemorating our time together, which was often spent drinking tea. Tea had become her staple drink in the last months of her life.

"When in 2012 would you like to travel, Mr. Dobbins?" I imagined an energetic bunny who at the sound of one note of "Jingle Bells" would leap from her chair in delight.

"I know it's the end of November, but by chance, are there any award seats available in December ... tomorrow?"

"Mr. Dobbins, please hold." I heard a slight snicker before the holiday music began to play.

I gazed at the second mug of tea I had poured in honor of Mom's departure. I'd set this honored tea with the mementos and stacks of condolence cards on her favorite table in the living room.

"Mr. Dobbins." The friendly, punctuated British accent

paused. "Well ... hmmm ... it seems there has been a cancellation for December 4. Would that work for you?" She seemed as puzzled and excited as I was.

*Was the Universe opening its doors with ease and grace? Was it synchronicity? Was it coincidence?*

"Mr. Dobbins, as long as I have worked for United ... to have an international cancellation ... " I heard her keyboard's tap, tap, click, click, and the holiday music turned to Kenny G, a jazz interpretation of "White Christmas."

"Let's book this now, before it gets away," she said, moving across the keyboard, a skater on ice. Reservations made.

I contacted the owner of Tidak Apa Apa, a Balinese homestead, and completed my online reservations. Over the next three days I packed and sent a few emails. I was ready for Bali, ready to heal.

I called my father in Missouri. "Son," he said, a long, deep pause, words moving from his belly, "you have been through so much, Eddie. You took care of your mother. You hear me?" I felt the peeling of the onion, raw, emotions resting, waiting for a gentle nudge to be released.

"Yes," I said, pressing mute on my phone between words, hiding the tears bubbling inside, like the Alka-Seltzer tablets I'd submerged in water.

"I am so proud, so very proud of you. How you handled

yourself and took care of your mother to her final breath. That is what a man, a son, is to do." I felt a choke of muscle tightening at the other end of the line. I recalled the weekly, sometimes daily, long-distance calls I'd made for his words of encouragement, laughter and biblical readings. He'd reminded me of how he, too, had watched over his mothers and sisters.

"Go to Bali. Call me when you get there. I love you."

"I love you too, Dad," I said in a caring tone that mirrored his support throughout the months.

He asked the Lord to protect me on my journey to Bali; he asked the Lord that I return home safely. He read aloud the prayer he kept folded in his Bible, that I had written for him from my home in Italy during the summer of 1997.

O Father
I sit in patience
Of your calling
On the Ocean's floor—
Sand prints;
The smell of cool air brushing
Against my wrapped body
Hidden from the Sun's light
The tingle of the wet currents
Splashing against the mounted

Boulder—erect with strength
Longevity.

O Father
I pray
Thy namesake
Faith and courage.
I sit here in silence
Meditating on words
Which leave me
Like the pains of the past;
Words of healing.

I am guided by the invisible
Awakened by the sounds
Of the Ocean's current's
A manifestation of your wonder
And your gifts.

O Father,
I am humbled for this moment
For the gifts of life and its authenticity.

O Father
I am human
A metamorphosis of thyself,

An image of creativity and beauty
Of bruises and scars—
Rebirth and resurrection.

O Father
I give thanks to thee
Like my brothers and sisters
Before me
The breadth of the invisible
Whispers of the Soul
You give life to.

O Father
I follow in your footsteps
Leading by the smiles of children's faces
Guided by a thread
Connecting me to the strength and power
Of your way.

O Father
I follow with courage and faith
Guided by the light
Sand prints into the Ocean
Infinite possibilities—

O Father
I sit here not as a child
But a man,
A man in your image—
Spirit—
Waiting, watching and waiting.

O Father
I sit here breathing with delight
Moved in spirit of tomorrow
While participating in the moment.

# CHAPTER 3

## I Rejoice in the Knowledge That
## We Are Truly All One

**Ubud – December 5, 2011**

Moving through Customs/Immigration, out into the canopy of tropical air, I feel alive, a sense of comfort, home, serenity. A cool breeze moves around me, though the air is hot and muggy. I am once again surrounded by the lure of Bali, a culture that maintains tradition and ritual amidst the flux and shifts of modern life.

I am met by a slender easygoing Balinese man, Nyoman. His coal black hair and cocoa complexion remind me of PJ ...

∽

I had met PJ in December of 1999 outside my office, the District Eight campaign headquarters for the re-election of Mayor Willie L. Brown, Jr., in San Francisco. The election was a historical moment in San Francisco politics, and my re-entry into the realities of day-to-day life upon my return from a trip around the world. The moment I saw

PJ, the cars moving up Castro and Upper Market Streets seemed suspended in air, released from their gravitational bondage. An electromagnetic pulse moved through my body, and I was certain Gilbert Baker's famous Rainbow Flag in the city's Castro District fluttered in happiness.

I mustered the courage to utter "hello" to this man about whom I had just imagined a full-scale love story. Was he the one?

Brown's political director had once said, "Remember, Dobbins, this is about turning out votes in December on Election Day." So it was my "duty" to meet the man I would come to know as PJ, to find out if he would be voting for Brown. PJ and I exchanged numbers and promised to connect in the New Year.

A few weeks later, after the celebratory election, I returned to Chicago to visit family for Christmas. Strolling through Walmart on the North Side of Chicago near Wicker Park with a friend, I saw PJ, pushing a metal cart down an aisle, the Pied Piper with a parade of women his age, all with strong familial resemblance, marching behind him. There I was, in a Walmart three thousand miles from San Francisco, two hours from my mother's home, following him down the aisle.

After many years of separating and coming together and separating again, he had reappeared in my life in June 2009. I hadn't seen him for nearly six years. I'd gotten used to his disappearances, his weaving in and out of my life. I had discovered that being involved with a man who was admired by many men and who had a husband at home was not something I wanted to fully explore.

PJ's periodic drive-bys were more sport than intimacy. After a long absence I'd encouraged him to interview for an Executive Director position with a San Francisco Institution where I was a trustee. Even though I sat on the interviewing panel, he was not able to influence the nine-member selection committee. We parted ways after this disappointment.

His "reappearance" in the form of a slender Balinese man was no coincidence.

∽

Nyoman and I make light conversation on the drive to the Balinese compound, as I look out on rows of rural homes piled next to rice fields. In small streams along the fields, villagers are dunking, dipping and washing under the moonlight. Gazebos, *bale bengongs,* were carefully placed in the rice fields, which were surrounded by bamboo forests.

Nyoman shares that the name of the house I will be staying in at the compound means "no worries, no problems," which he jokes also means "putting one's head into the sand." *How perfect,* I think as we drive through the dark with only the moonlight as our guide. I repeat to myself silently, "No worries, no problems."

On roughly three hectares, hidden behind a thick brick wall is a family compound in the shape of the human body, with a rectangle of walls around its perimeter. The body of the compound lies on the *kaja-kelod* line (representing upstream/divine and downstream/negative forces), facing the mountain on one side and the ocean on the other, eight degrees below the equator. I had decided not to stay in a hotel surrounded by strangers; instead I chose the compound so I could feel part of a family and community.

My home for the next fourteen days is tucked away behind the family compound. Surrounded by a wall, with a private entrance, it will be a perfect place to recharge, and only three kilometers from the center of Ubud. The compound is designed to keep out unwanted demons. Uneven brick steps lead to the rustic bronze gate of the compound, with a small brick temple shrine at the entrance. Scattered Jepun petals delicately pave the entranceway. Landscaped gardens lined with trees and colorful flowers are throughout the property. Incense sticks and palm leaf trays sprinkled with cooked rice are used for daily ritual to the gods. The sweet aroma of the Jepun flowers carry me through a dark brick maze to the two-story bungalow tucked behind a second five-foot brick wall—this is my home. The privacy and beauty of the place give me a deep sense of serenity.

"Tidak Apa Apa" (no worries, no problems), written in white and black pebbles embedded in circular patterns created from more white and black pebbles, like the intricate designs on the famed coastal sidewalks of Rio de Janeiro, leads toward the lower apartment's front entrance. I choose the second-level apartment, which I call the "green room," for it seems quiet and above the fray, and offers a spacious suite with a surrounding view.

Jet-lagged from the thirty-two-hour journey from Chicago to Honk Kong, Singapore and finally the Denpasar International Airport in Indonesia, I shower and jump into bed. I lay listening to a chorus of male voices singing, chanting Ramayana (a Hindu monkey chant) from the Dalem Temple down the road.

## December 7, 2011

There is a gentle knock at my door. A muffled vibration moves through the carved wooden door. I am frightened by the sound, or perhaps by my heartbeat, like I am of the green creatures, the geckos, crawling on the ceiling over my head.

"Mr. Eddie," a voice whispers from outside the door.

*Am I dreaming? Am I still in prayer? Was it HER?*

I move across the white marble tiles in my white athletic socks, but I do not go to the door. I ignore the knock and the voice. The geckos, blending in with the bamboo tapestry, watch in silence, unsure of what I might do next. What they see is not yoga. It is not meditation. Instead it's a church revival with hollering. Is it a routine of sorts? Is it prayer?

The geckos and Hindu gods witness this act of bhakti, an homage to faith and love. They witness a man in a trance, a soul hosting spirits and deities in sacred force in the material world. An acoustic guitar rests in one corner of the room next to a five-gallon bottle water dispenser. A wooden armoire with assorted books left by guests, perches in another corner. The queen-size bed is flanked by two bedside tables, a sofa/futon, a computer desk, and most importantly, a western toilet. I swirl on the tile floor, spinning like a spun top, then stand glued to the spot. I'm on my hands and knees. I stretch my legs out from underneath my torso and sit, hands clasped, each extended finger touching the other.

I pray. I pray to the Hindu gods, to Buddha, to Moses and Abraham. I pray and shout the name of Jesus. I spew every prayer I know, safe in the cocoon of my Balinese house, geckos and gods viewing me from above. I lovingly hold the white handkerchief embroidered with a red heart with the initial "e," for Eddie Senior, inside it, a gift from my father to my mother. I hold this cloth to my heart and am reminded of the *kajang,* a roll of white cloth, filled with sacred drawings and letters that in Balinese ritual is the last object to be placed on the deceased for entry to the next life.

I summon all spirits: "PLEASE COME NOW!"

Her death hits me all at once! A wet wrung-out towel, spun into a coiled cylinder, tightens in my intestines. The calm, cool, collected yoga-meditating self takes the punch, a ripping, twisting punch to the gut. The grief descends through me, through my feet into the ground.

Like a cyclone, swirling and whistling as it increases in velocity, I am angry! I am angry with my mother's daughter. *Why did she participate with such indifference?* I am angry with my mother for not putting her affairs in order. There is no way to deny the disastrous financial situation I have been left to attend to. I am depressed to my core.

"Mr. Eddie?" A calm voice from the other side of the door whispers again.

I sheepishly shuffle to the door, while the geckos take shelter like children playing hide-and-seek. I open it a crack.

Standing there is a spindly woman with an olive/nut-brown complexion. Her ink-black hair is pulled back into a ponytail, highlighting her light brown eyes and Cupid's bow lips, parched from the sun. She gives a glimpse of teeth, then breaks into an infectious smile. There is a fragileness to her stance, yet her whole being resonates ease and cheerful exuberance.

"Welcome to Bali," she says as the sun peeks through from behind her. Her greeting is warm and familiar, her gentle gaze accepting and kind. As she opens the door wider, I see through the window in the hallway to where chickens, dogs and pigs scurry through the garden below. Temple bells ring, a background sonata of romance piercing the jungle canopy, streaming through my open door. Peering onto the landscape from above, I imagine the morning dew dancing and dripping from the golden rice in the fields just beyond the compound. A silhouette of holy shrines emerges from the morning mist as I peer over the tiled roofs.

"My name is Kadek," she says happily, her arms unfolding to encompass my waist, her head meeting my chin. This cuddly gesture is wrapped in hidden fragrances.

"Thank you," I say as I easily return her embrace.

Her hug is motherly and strong. She has earned her living through her hands, and she reminds me of my grandmother, Ida Beach, who picked cotton in the fields of the South.

"Please come downstairs. I have special Balinese breakfast for you." Her face, devoid of makeup, unleashes a child's joy. Her dress is Western: jeans and a pullover shirt, reflecting island attire for *pembantu* (house director). Butterflies fly freely through the white scent of hibiscus, aster, roses and hydronium, all woven together.

She moves down the cement stairs with the delicate joy of a Balinese dancer. Familiar with each hand-molded concrete-block step, she reflects serenity.

I follow her and sit in a bamboo rocking chair on the marble landing of the lower terrace. I take in the view of orchids, palm trees with coconuts and my favorite flowering plant, the Javanese Ixora, with its large round clusters of bright red and orange blossoms. Rich baritone chimes echo from nearby temples.

Green pots filled with white flowers are placed symmetrically in front of each stone column on the landing. A Hindu clay statue of a monkey is the focal point of the garden, and black and white checkered flags strung between the columns flutter in the cool, damp morning breeze. I'm daydreaming as I breathe in the beauty around me, flirting with each magical impression.

"Is there anything you need?" Kadek asks.

"Please join me," I say, gesturing to the rocking chair on the other side of the table.

After a simple quiet blessing, I pour Kadek a cup of the black, Indonesian oolong tea she brought me when I first sat down. Tiny specs of tea, once leaves, now crushed, swirling in slow suspended motion, conjoining the spirit, wisdom, strength and delight of two human beings, the yin (female energy) and the yang (male energy).

Our conversation begins intimately. Through broken stumbling vowels, Kadek shares the challenges of raising a family in Bali. She shares her dreams of seeing her children, Gary and Maya, get a secondary school education. She tells how she met her husband, Made. With delight, she talks about her brother, mother and father, all living in the village of Tabanan, where the revolutionary hero Ngu Rai once lived.

"Ubud, very special," she says, as she sips from the teacup, holding it with both hands. "There is magic here." She looks at me with intensity. "Is this your first time to Bali?"

"No, this is my second time. I was here in June of 2009 for a month holiday."

She is pleased that I wanted to return, and asks lovingly, "What brings you to paradise this time?"

I share briefly that I have come for healing, to write through my grieving.

"Who died?" she asks lightly, bluntly, as she looks into my eyes. She sees the raw sensitivity, that I am still reeling from death, my knees folded in the chair, my body hunched slightly forward. I feel Kadek's love, her empathy, in her soft brown eyes. I also feel peace and serenity.

"My mother." I'm holding my matching teacup firmly in one hand, balancing the piece of toast I was savoring in my other hand. The bread is soft and delicate, spread with honey and preserved apricots. "I've come to Bali to explore, unwind and write," I explain with a sense of hope as well as resolution.

She looks sad and lowers her eyes toward her lap.

"Do you pray?"

"Yes." I am thinking of how I started my pre-sleep routine, upon my arrival, in the green room, a few hours earlier.

"I pray every morning, not because I have to. I need to," Kadek explains. "It's in my blood. Prayer is very important here. We pray for many things."

Her experience of prayer seems to echo my own.

"I born here." She pauses. "I talk to my gods every day. They listen." She looks at me. "I know I am a Balinese. I am from Ubud." She smiles with conviction. She has my attention. "Your mother here with you now." She looks at me with knowing eyes. Is she sensing something I am not? *Is Kadek the answer to my prayer?*

"Today, what your plan?" she asks as she begins to gather the empty dishes. She places them on a tray, one by one, with a steadiness, a flow of careful consideration.

"I have no plans, other than doing some writing," I say, feeling jet-lagged and stuffed, but grateful for an amazing meal. I am eager to explore my surrounding, eager to breathe.

"What you writing?"

We watch as a young woman in a bright orange, red and green sarong carries rice and flowers on a small woven tray made of palm leaves. She walks mysteriously in silence. Smoke from lit incense guards her privacy. She begins to pray, blessing the evil spirits away with eyes closed, her right hand clutching a bundle of flowers. With a flick of her wrist, she dips the bundle three times.

"Beautiful," Kadek remarks, noticing how closely I am taking in this morning ritual. This simple prayer is done throughout the day across the entire island.

"What you write?" she asks again. The burning jasmine and rose petal incense blows in our direction, then disappears in the thick humidity.

"I am writing about my 203 days as a caregiver," I respond.

"Beautiful," she whispers. "You're a writer?"

As I hold on to her question, like a kite, a bird ascending, wings spread to the clouds, a cosmic message to the gods, I dip back in time, remembering a version of Kadek's question from Gwendolyn Elizabeth Brooks, a Poet Laureate of Illinois, when I told her my dream to be a writer. A dream hidden in pages, words and syllables, caged, neatly stored away.

When I met Brooks in March of 1981, as a junior at Oak Park and River Forest High School in Oak Park, Illinois, I was captivated. She took command of the large auditorium filled to capacity. She spoke in a grandmother-ly voice wrapped in deep tones that reflected her Southern roots, slowly and methodically: "Poetry is looking at life, the way it really is and reporting on it ... Write about everything, not just flowers and spring time, but what you really think and feel. Write about your bicycle, about war, or McDonald's hamburgers ... I believe in writing from experience, but observation is a legitimate aspect of experience." The *Oak Park-River Forest Journal* reported excerpts of her speech that day.

She encouraged us as black kids, but strongly and in-clusively brought everyone together that morning, to in-spire each of us to find solace in words, as she did.

I was invited to lunch with Ms. Brooks and a few oth-er students after the assembly. She was a black celebrity in my mind, a living legend. She had been raised on the South Side of Chicago. I devoured her poetry—simple words with complex undertones.

Her words remain tucked away in a kaleidoscope of memories, carefully woven patterns, delicately shaped. The memory a reminder to put my dreams, fears and joys into words. To craft and capture words on paper, like a photographer documenting life through the lens of a cam-era.

Kadek notices me slip away. "What would you call your book?" she asks.

The playful laughter of two young children running in the garden on the other side of the wall creates an embracing harmony. Their words provoke a memory of my mother's directions for making her Lipton tea. It was labeled and boxed in containers, some with sturdy metal clasps. She boasted that black tea gave her a lift that supported her delicate immune system. It provided me, too, with a boost of energy, a release from stress. Her white tea, stored on the counter next to her spices, had a hand-printed crumpled yellow sticky-note planted inside, labeled "For Cancer."

"Use the glass cup, run the tap water for a bit, not too cold, not too hot. Fill the glass, place it in the microwave, press 'Beverage' and watch the timer to 50 seconds. Then place a decaffeinated Lipton teabag into the glass in the microwave. Make sure you push the teabag into the water, restart the microwave, press 'Beverage,' let sit for a minute. Then you will have a perfect cup of tea."

Laughing inwardly, I respond to Kadek's question. *"Tea with Mom."* Kadek looks as pleased with the title as I am.

As Brooks said: "Write about everything, not just flowers and spring time, but what you really think and feel." Perhaps that is why I have returned to Bali, to think and feel.

After eating every morsel of food on my plate, I return to my upstairs room to pack for a move to the blue room downstairs, for relief from the noisy feet of the geckos. One thing I discovered in the green room was that the world of geckos didn't end. The interlayered bamboo rafters over my bed had been moving during the night as tiny green feet scratched like toothpicks, razors, across a blackboard. Geckos had clung to the ceiling, blending in with its color.

When I was in Bali in June 2009 I had stayed at a resort overlooking a portion of the seventy-five kilometer Ayung River. I moved to three different rooms in a span of eight days. Sleep deprived, I wondered why I had chosen Bali, when Italy would have been easier to get to.

My first night on the island of paradise, I had nestled in my suite, luxuriating in six-hundred-thread-count cotton sheets. Jasmine scent wafted through the seven-hundred-square-foot living space. A dark wooden armoire with a matching chest of drawers and other tasteful antique furnishings filled the space. Paintings of the river, with views of Mount Agung and Mount Batur and rice fields dotted with farmers bent over planting, graced the room.

I remember dropping into bed, snuggling in contentment with toes curled in pleasure. I nestled like a newborn baby. In unison, an orchestra of green lizards peered at me from the ceiling. Their eyes glowed like lightning bugs in the darkness.

Desperately frightened of being eaten alive by what

seemed like hundreds if not thousands of lizards, I jumped onto the middle of my bed with a flashlight in one hand and phone in the other. Dropping the phone and pressing its buttons with my big toe—a skill I had practiced in my head in case of emergencies—I managed to summon three security officials.

I could see their lights waving and bouncing off the trees and hear the whistling of branches and stomping of twigs as they came running one by one to my rescue. The sound of lions coming through the jungle. The water in a pool just outside my sliding glass doors reflected the bouncing beam of the flashlight in my shaking hands. *Do I call the American Consulate? Will I be eaten alive?*

Three men stood in front of the glass door, pointing their flashing lights toward the creatures. "American on holiday," I saw in their tiger eyes. In a chorus of falling notes, the "Three Tenors," not in black tuxedos but in matching batik short-sleeve shirts and beige khakis, sang out a harmony of hysterics. I was not amused. They laughed their way into my room, patting each other on the back, and I knew that by morning my incident with the green creatures would be shared with their fellow workers across the compound.

"Mr. Eddie," one of them said, "geckos are a good thing." He explained that I would not die. They swooshed the three geckos out of the room (yes, there were only three) but I slept nervously, counting geckos instead of sheep.

In my new room, Kadek presents me with a binder of tourist information. "There beautiful things to see in Bali," she says. "While you were moving to your new home, I pray, this is what the gods ... " She holds out a scrap of brown paper, a piece of a paper cone used for rice dishes served by street vendors.

I take it from her hand in a delicate motion, feeling gratitude, and read the words scribbled in English:

Monkey Forest Temple

Mother Temple

Tanah Lot Sacred Temple

*Is Kadek a messenger of sorts?* I remember times when I have followed my intuition and discovered great adventure. My nose is captivated by the lit incense and mix of succulent aromas. I am struck that both Agung and Kadek have mentioned Monkey Forest—the Temple of Death.

# CHAPTER 4

# I Balance My Openness to the Universe

### Ubud – December 8, 2011

I stroll down Jalan Sri Wedari, passing the Dalem Temple, on my way to the Temple of Death. I walk aimlessly, surrounded by golden glimmering needles of rice growing in the distance around old and new wooden structures. I step over streams of suds flowing over freshly sprayed sidewalks, out onto the road and toward the jungle. I peer into friendly faces and smile as we greet each other. The buildings seem to blend into the quiet surroundings. I retrace the steps I took when I walked this road in 2009.

Jalan Sri Wedari, uneven, part dirt, part paved, leads to the south, to Jalan Raya Ubud, the main thoroughfare in and out of Ubud. On Jalan Raya Ubud, I pass Nomad Café. The aromas of seared tuna and roasted garlic, the delicate scent of shredded raw shallots, chilies and garlic waft through the street, though the Ubud Art Market, following me all the way to Jalan Monkey Forest. Horns beep and mopeds whiz by, drivers occasionally stopping to ask, "Do you need a ride, mister?" A breeze whips up light golden kernels of rice particles, which fall like snow from the sky. It is December, after all.

I pass familiar stores like Yanvan, a silversmith and jewelry design shop. "Welcome back to Ubud, Mr. Eddie!" Three sales clerks who waited on me in 2009 are still there, where I purchased an expensive thick silver ring as a graduation gift to myself.

At the entrance to Monkey Forest, I am greeted by a crab-eating Macaque monkey with short rugged arms and legs and a long sturdy tail used for balance and jumping. His upper torso is brown with golden-tipped fur, his feet and ears are black, his muzzle a light greyish pink. I feel at home, as he checks me over and gives me a nod, indicating I'm okay to enter.

Moving through the sacred forest, I see beasts peering from all corners, swinging, watching from above. Are they leading me to motherly love? Passing ancient trees and Hindu temple complexes, I finally find the Temple of Death. Not at all as I imagined it—grand and glorious with trumpets blaring. It is simple yet somehow majestic.

The Temple of Death holds a mystical power that compels the Balinese through the forest to worship at its altar. Here I am connecting to my ancestral spirits and the gods, all of whom move me to worship. I am led by invisible powers. I can feel, taste, smell and touch the mystery, the ancient Balinese medicine.

With hands firmly in my lap, I sit in solitude, concentrating on the sound of my breath, and I move into deep contentment, aligned with the natural world around me. I am in the presence of unquestionable tranquility. The sacred words "Om Mani Padme Om" move through me, anchoring me to the earth like the roots of a banyan tree. Sounds vibrate within every cell of my body, activating my senses, my awakening. The rustling of leaves gently surrounds me, and the breeze pushes me as the sun shifts and glows through the canopy of green. The grace and beauty around me remind me of her departure.

I shift back in time to grammar school, to a moment when meditation and prayer became an anchor that allowed me to move through difficult experiences. Without expectation or judgments, without a running mental commentary on my process, these experiences delivered moment-by-moment awareness. The opportunity to pray was presented to me in the form of impetigo, debilitating asthma, allergies to milk, grass, mold, eggs. I meditated for survival, without knowing what I was doing.

My body shook like the red school bell that was buzzing, anchored high on the outdoor wall. Third-graders rushed inside from the blacktop-covered, brick-enclosed playground, skidding across the marble floors. Recess was over. In the distance a fire truck screamed down Jeffrey Boulevard. I stood at the entrance for a moment, daydreaming of being on the red truck. Finally I walked through the gigantic door, stepping lightly in my black Converse gym shoes. I carried the red ball we used for playing kickball and dodge ball.

The red school bell bellowed. I dribbled the ball down the hallway toward the classroom. Mrs. Robinson, a lanky, dark-skinned woman, stood in the hallway hurrying us to our destinations. It was March and the snow was melting, so unzipped jackets hung open, revealing cotton crewneck sweaters. The odor of liverwurst, cheese, peanut butter and chips hung like a cloud in the halls and classrooms. My nose rebelled.

As I entered the classroom Mrs. Robinson grabbed the ball from my hands. She peered at me, her eyes large and round like marbles reflecting fire. "You are a worthless child!" Her loud words flew past me and stuck to the chalkboard behind me. In a lowered voice she snarled, "One day God will punish you for having a white mother."

∽

The stillness in the forest urges me to vocalize the vibrating syllables of Om Mani Padme Om to unleash the buried grief that is surfacing. Memories of motherly love surround me at the Temple of Death. I am coming alive in the jungle, sensing ancient mystical vibrations moving through me. Currents of sound, howls, birds flapping, scents of dew and dirt, the aliveness of the critters buried deep in the foliage awaken me to the motherly love residing inside me. Eyes closed, breath slow and rhythmic, I imagine all my concerns vanish into nothingness as my body relaxes. I am serene, embodying the spirit of the forest, untangling memories. An intense love and peace radiate from the sky. A beam of white light bathes and purifies my soul, and I release the unwanted energy of death and of 203 days of caregiving into an abyss of love.

"Does this suffering have meaning?" I write across the page of the journal I have opened on my lap. The words look back at me as a small parade of Balinese women glide past me, praying in unison.

"Will my faith sustain me? What am I suffering?"

"Why, Eddie, do you call it suffering?" Agung's words float to the surface as I sip the remaining water from the plastic bottle I brought with me.

*Motherly love. What is motherly love? Is it an act of being? Is it kindness? Is it turning darkness into light?*

❧

I return to Tidak Apa Apa. The compound is quiet except for faint gibberish emanating from a small television set in someone's room. In my blue room I change into lightweight pajamas and sit on the porch of my bungalow with my journal. I tear out a blank piece of paper and print, writing each letter in a deliberate attempt to dissolve my pain: "You are a worthless child. One day God will punish you for having a white mother."

I walk into the garden, following the steps of the young girl I saw earlier. I recite aloud the Peace Prayer of Saint Francis of Assisi:

> Lord, make me an instrument of your peace:
> where there is hatred, let me sow love;
> where there is injury, pardon;
> where there is doubt, faith;
> where there is despair, hope;
> where there is darkness, light;
> where there is sadness, joy.

> O Divine Master,
> grant that I may not so much seek
> to be consoled, as to console;
> to be understood, as to understand;
> to be loved, as to love.
> For it is in giving that we receive,
> It is in pardoning that we are pardoned,
> and it is in dying that we are born to eternal life.

Mrs. Robinson's words, cocooned in the fabric of my DNA, now spark into flames on a ceremonial tray of palm leaves. I feel a canopy open, allowing me to expand. I look up at a night sky of stars bursting in every direction. I speak to my Higher Power: "I release this limiting belief, this misinterpretation of reality, and every belief, attitude and behavior spawned from this misbelief, for the very last time." The words disappear as the paper dissolves into ash, into the nothingness from which they came.

For two rainy days I stay in my room and tell Kadek that I will not be needing any service. Instead, I prepare my own small meals and order delivery pizza from town. Between watching the dozen or so DVDs in my room, I think about the time I spent taking care of my mother.

On the third day the sun beams through the open curtains. I peek out from the black sleeping mask from Singapore Airlines and notice a faint shadow, a movement, through the window out to the deck.

Kadek is quietly sweeping; the sound of bristly straw on the slick marble tile creates a soothing rhythm.

"Good morning, Kadek," I say as I open the window.

"Good morning." She smiles wide. "You okay?"

"I'm fine." I brush the sleep from my eyes and look at the mess I have created over two days in hibernation.

"You *left* your room?" she asks, looking puzzled, wondering why someone would travel halfway around the world to stay shuttered in a room watching movies. But I knew that she knew.

"You order pizza in Bali? I stop now ... I go make you special Balinese food from the gods." She glides across the floor toward the kitchen without waiting for my response. The kitchen takes up two rooms in the south of the compound. It contains a five-foot refrigerator, two electric burners, a microwave, and spices lined against one wall and sealed to keep out critters.

After a long hot shower, I change into shorts and T-shirt. I open my front door to see the bamboo coffee table overflowing with food. On it sits an urn of fresh Indonesian black tea, Nasi Goreng—shredded chicken on a bed of rice, green beans, peppers and mushrooms—and two pieces of toast made from fresh-baked bread and served with homemade marmalade, plus two eggs over-easy. I devour the meal.

On the lower step of the veranda, Kadek appears with an offering of various fruits indigenous to the island. She observes me with the eyes of a mother.

"You like?" she asks in her high-pitched voice. She sees how her food from the gods has affected my mood.

"Wonderful, Kadek, simply wonderful!" I am still

relishing the sweetness of the blended peppers in the Nasi Goreng.

"What's you plan?" she asks.

"I am going to the Mother Temple today."

"Ahhhh ... Mother Temple. Do you go to other temple?" She asks like a mother checking to see if her child has paid attention.

"Yes, I'm going on a private tour for the day." I'm excited for the journey and what might be revealed for healing.

"Good!" she exclaims, as she disappears into the kitchen. "Enjoy your day. See you in the morning!" Then she calls out: "I have special gift for you. Be here at 8 A.M. tomorrow. We leave at 8:30 A.M. on motorbike. Okay?"

I understand this isn't a question, but a firm plan.

# CHAPTER 5

# I Am Grateful for All the Beauty Around Me

**Ubud – December 11, 2011**

As our car ascends slowly through curving passes, we hear the sounds of the *kulkul*, a Balinese wooden slit gong, a musical instrument used to summon the gods. We move up a long road, turn a sharp corner, and there she is, Pura Besakih—the Mother Temple—an architectural wonder mirroring the structures of the Gelgel Dynasty. She is perched a thousand meters above sea level, built on the slope of Mount Agung, and is part of an enormous complex of smaller temples.

My driver drops me at the entrance, allowing me to wander alone. I feel something stirring inside me. I feel like Rocky Balboa, standing on the first step, looking up. I imagine the hands, the lives, the sacrifice it took to build this wonder.

Children strategically huddled in small packs offer items for purchase. "Mister, you buy postcard," insists a girl with outstretched hand, pleading eyes and dirty feet.

Vendors selling chilled bottled water are stationed at every few steps. Women, children, hands reaching, eyes and mouths asking for money.

I begin to climb the stairs. Panoramic images of memories swirl in the dust storm moving around me. *Are Brahma, Vishnu and Shiva present?*

I find a quiet spot and close my eyes, shifting into a silent mediation. I focus on my breath. When I sense a presence, I open my eyes. A young man stands before me, in a long white robe with a black sash.

He rests a hand on my shoulder. A heat pours through his palm, a frequency of energy. I can smell him—all of him—dry, damp, musky.

"Hello, brother," he says softly. He reaches for my hand and pulls me up from my spot on the stairs. The strength in his arm and his grip captivate me. I feel suddenly reborn by his kindness.

I also feel physically taunted. A test? A gift? He challenges me without needing to say much. Through touch I am moved. Our eyes connect. We are the same height. Tenderness and strength stand before me, like a delicate root. Have we met before, in a different lifetime … lovers?

He holds my hand, our fingers interlocking. His unsubtle strength anchors me. We walk in silence, each step in unison … soldiers. I feel strangely shielded, like we are the only two people in existence, yet many tourists surround us. I feel at home in his presence.

Holding his callous-free brown hand, my muscles tighten. I am awakened. No agenda. I savor each step, each movement providing intimate excitement. The silent space between us echoes and captivates me. I surrender, physically, spiritually. Will I be falling into the arms of a stranger?

He leads me up the magnificent steps, taking each one slowly. We walk through an ancient kingdom of mysteries, rituals, magic. We find our way to the highest elevation, to a huge temple closed to the public. He opens the gate with his key, which dangles on a string on his coiled black rope sash. He leads us, me, back in time, to an altar enclosed by large bronze gates.

This temple priest walks me to an area used for birth and death ceremonies. *A temple of life and death.* He holds a wooden hand-carved goblet decorated in bright golds, containing fresh water from the holy spring blessed by the gods. He looks at me with a seriousness I have not yet seen, and with three casual flicks of his hand, sprinkles water into the air. It is like the striking of a match, or the conductor at an orchestra's first measure.

He mumbles a prayer in Sanskrit:

*Om Bhur Bhuvah Swaha;*
*Tat Savitur Varenyam Bhargo Devasya Dhimahi;*
*Dhiyo Yonah Pracodayat.*
*Om. Santih. Santih, Santih.*
(Body of all. Mind of all. Spirit of all.
May we meditate on the radiance of the inner light.
May that self illuminate our thoughts.
Peace. Peace. Peace.)

He guides me to take three sips of the holy water. He drips a little into my connected palms, then gently places bits of cooked rice on my third eye, in the middle of my forehead, between my brows, to aid the process of my awakening. I embrace the elaborateness of this unfamiliar ritual. I feel a resonance of merged cultures.

We sit together, shoulders touching. His energy connects me to the earth as the sun shields us. Facing the altar, he holds my hand and says another prayer to the gods. His gentle touch moves my blood from the tips of my toes to the vortex of my head, unearthing and releasing the dark clouds hovering inside.

∽

When I was five or six years old, I dreamed my paternal grandmother had passed away.

"Mommy, how's Grandma?" I casually asked.

"She's fine."

A few hours later, I heard my mother whispering into the yellow rotary phone with the loops of its cord stretched across the room.

"No, you tell him."

"Little Eddie," my father said, "my mother passed early this morning. Your grandmother."

"Where did she go?" I asked.

He didn't explain. Still, I seemed to comprehend what death meant. Perhaps she went to the same place my parrot Mikey, named after Michael Jackson, had gone. Mikey was perched on a small wooden bar in his cage one day while Michael belted out "Rockin' Robin." At the place in the song where there are many "tweets," Mikey tweeted along to the point of a heart attack, and fell to the floor of his metal cage. Mikey was buried in a shoebox. Death explained.

Dreams continued to be a source of guidance for me, showing up in the physical world in the form of unexplained coincidences. Like when I happened to walk into a bookstore, because it was on my path, and then walked directly to an area where I saw a book fall to the floor. I picked it up and noticed it was by Krishnamurti. I opened to a random page and read:

"Each of us as a human being must bring about a radical revolution in himself ... The search for truth and the questions as to whether there is a God, will be answered by nobody, but yourself ... Take a journey and find a state of mind which is never in conflict ... you can only see truth when the mind is not fragmented, when you see the totality. You can only look totally when you give your whole attention without fear."

This quote helped clarify my decision to take an around-the-world journey in 1997, and has continued to be a guiding light when I feel stuck or timid.

In the summer of 1997, Italy became my home and a place where answers to my existential questions began to reveal themselves. Italy was also where my writing, meditating and inner work began to take shape. As my inner work began, so did my shift in consciousness. My relationship with myself and others changed; it felt more spontaneous, natural, effortless. The question of God's existence plagued me and led me in the discovery of sacred spiritual gifts.

Letting go proved to be the gateway to spirituality for me. Letting go was not an overnight success. I learned it is a process, like peeling delicate layers of an onion, relinquishing control, while letting creative energies in. I allowed myself to be led into a state of flow with life, which heightened my awareness. I felt connected to a universal life force.

The rapids of fear touch me again as I sit in the temple; they knock me off my game. My life, in embracing the death of my mother, has been shattered. Will I face financial ruin? Has my fragile health been jeopardized? Am I afraid of really living?

A peacefulness moves through me. The energy of the priest remains idle, hovering in space without words. I am in the presence of death.

The priest encourages me to pray. He leaves me alone, giving me space to grieve. Hands clasped, I pray for guidance. I pray for gratitude. I pray for my family, my friends and humanity.

In deep reflective prayer, surrounded by the silent beauty of the ancient temple, a magic swirling, images bouncing, birds darting in circles around me, incense burning. Tantalizing. *Is spirit present?*

> "By thy hand, must all be fed,
> give us Lord our daily bread.
> By thy hand, must all be fed,
> give us Lord our daily bread. Amen."

"THE ROOM!" The words bounce off the temple walls and reverberate in my head.

Shish, shish, shish. Slowly, methodically ... the silent power of nylons rasping, rubbing together like two sand blocks. Tick tock, tick tock—the sound of her shoes hitting the floor with precision. Manicured from neck to waist, with a removable apron, her dress hitting her calves, cream-colored pantyhose encasing her thick thighs, white socks showing above black orthopedic shoes. Her bold, plump frame emanated discipline.

"The room" on the second level, hidden behind swinging doors, was her sewing room. It was plain: a bed and a nightstand with a big black book as the centerpiece.

I stood in the corner of the sewing room on one leg. My punishment. She sat patiently on her hard bed, on its gray army fabric bedspread. The wooden paddle, the length of a forearm, was secured to her wrist by a rubber loop. Even a slight touch of my toe to the floor would provoke a swipe of the paddle. It seemed the punishment might last for hours.

A religious woman in her late sixties, Alberta knew what it was like to be black in America. She was determined, that evening, to make sure I knew, too. After a long time the punishment ended and she directed me to sit next to her. She showed me her Bible, read a few verses, then closed the book and began to pray. She prayed that I would lead the other children, for they looked up to me, she said; she prayed that I would learn how to pray. She prayed that I would stay in my bed.

She clasped my hands together. I knelt beside her. My elbows rested on the tightly tucked bed, my legs ached in pain. My head bent slightly; hovering over the gray blanket, I began to pray. I prayed in silence; I prayed out loud. I even prayed to be less of a problem for her and the others.

Through prayer, I learned a valuable tool for survival at "The Home."

❦

The young priest reappears, his timing impeccable.

"Mr. Eddie," he says, his voice tender. I sit motionless, unraveling thoughts of The Home.

"How you feel?" he asks gingerly, the swooping sound of the "ee" floating toward the open sky. He reaches for my hands, pulling me close for comfort.

"You have a beautiful soul," he whispers. My forehead glistens from the sun's heat. His innocence is natural, unassuming, the peppermint scent of his breath inviting.

"You have a beautiful soul," I whisper, as I grab a hanky from my back pocket. We smile. Entwined in a gaze of love and surrender.

"Your blessings here are from the gods." He gestures

toward the open gate where the pinnacle of Mount Agung is visible above the clouds—the blessing.

"Thank you. Really, thank you. I feel the energy and the magic here."

"Where do you stay?" he asks as we make a slow descent from the temple.

"Ubud," I say, sounding like a seasoned traveler.

"Ahh, beautiful. You are in the cultural hub of my country," he says with pride and perfect English. He makes sure I watch each step as we descend. "Is this your first time to Bali?" he asks, knowing it isn't.

"No, it's my second. There is something here in Bali that moves me. I feel so at peace here." I want to know more about my host. "Where do you live?" I ask.

"I live here, this is my village. My family, we all born here. I am part of that mountain and that mountain is part of me. My wife and three children are just ten minutes away," he says with a fatherly glow.

"Three children!" I say with surprise. He looks so young. "How old are you?" I ask.

"I am twenty-nine." He smiles with a seductive smirk. "Beautiful!"

We reach the base level of temples and say goodbye like old friends—we embrace, shake hands and hug, twice.

"I'll see you next time in Bali," he says. *Does he know something I don't?*

"Until then." I hold my right hand over my heart in a gesture of love and gratitude.

~

During the car ride back to the compound, I slip away to early July 2009. I was celebrating my return to America from my first trip to Bali, along with my master's degree and a new job. I'd hit the ground running!

While traveling coast to coast as Vice President of Channel Development for a San Francisco startup, I regularly spoke with my mother between flights. Her answers to my general questions—"How are you?" "How do you feel?" "Is there anything you need?"—provided me with enough information to gather the state of her health, and then to tune into mine.

My home was on the north slope of Potrero Hill, the southern tip of San Francisco. A five-unit building with views of Twin Peaks, downtown and the Bay Bridge had been rebuilt into a single-family home with separate living spaces for five people. It stood four stories high with nearly five thousand square feet of total living space. It was steps away from a corridor of trendy shops and restaurants.

My flat was an eight-hundred-square-foot living space with built-in floor-to-ceiling cherry designer cabinetry along one wall. Recessed lights lined a small carpeted area that provided comfort to bare feet, as did the heated flooring in the kitchen and bathroom.

The foundation of the home was dug deep into the earth. It provided solid support for the building during earthquakes, and for me. This foundation also supported my connection with PJ.

He returned to my life on April 28, 2009: "Dear Eddie: Just ran into your picture on FB. I am sorry that we've lost touch. I miss your friendship and am glad to know you are well. Please write back if you get a chance. I am back in Chicago. All the best, PJ."

I responded: "I am in receipt of your message and had to sit with it for a bit—an array of emotions surfaced and moved me gently to a very quiet place to 'process'—I have missed you from my life the moment you drove away that evening from the Embarcadero parking lot. I am often in Chicago, for my mother is transitioning and I'm trying to spend as much time with her as possible before she leaves physical world reality. Although I prefer to speak live at some point—just wanted to say hello and respond to your thoughtful connection. All the best, Eddie."

Was the Universe bringing two men together, so each one could cable into the other as Source, as energy, for their own healing?

❧

"I miss you," he said. Three simple words twining their way to my ears through the phone. Three words that moved through every muscle, membrane, cell. *Was I his rebound? Or something else entirely? Something I had yet to understand?*

"I miss you," I said, knowing every ounce of me would warm to his touch, his breath. His voice rang with sexual gasps that looped, pulled, hooked … a tango … I waited in anticipation, moving silently through my apartment.

A yellow cab pulled up, a door opened, a door closed. I saw him move, swagger the way he did, a man, a boy, on a journey; the streetlight paved his way. The doorbell rang. Was this a prayer? A vision? A wish? A lesson?

His smirk was familiar. We embraced like two men who had been lost, returning home.

Our lips touched, slowly, as strangers; our footsteps moved closer. A slow motion of anticipation and memories. Our eyes danced in the flickering light of a candle in the hallway. Shadows of our silent dance. Our hands touched, similar in length, strength and structure. Olive-toned. A warmth melted the air between us, an extended vibration reaching into a quiet place of deep trust, of strength, where in the moment I felt a vitality, a rushing heat. My hands moved from his waist up his back.

Through his leather jacket I could feel his ribs. I could smell his breath, his thick black hair. Was he home?

His whispered "I missed you" stopped my heart.

His embrace followed, with confidence. Two souls intertwined in complete grace of movement; I craved this rhythm of connection. My breath sent smoke signals—a two-syllable name in the heat of the night. The brush of his fingers over my lips, like a painter priming his canvas.

He had brought me an autographed copy of his book. "I never cease to be amazed at how the grand author continues to weave our lives—glad that you are part of the journey."

Was he a reflection of my perception? Did he, or I, project a sense of inadequacy on the other? Did we participate in our own objectification, or engage in behavior or thoughts that were damaging? Did he objectify or mistreat me, or use me for his own pleasure and purpose—knowing he would never love me?

I moved through his book, a ribbon of words that took me on a journey through his past relationships toward his personal healing. I was thrilled to read each page. I was an audience taking in the calligraphy of sounds through the lyrics of his soul ... the soul of a man who had walked away from me. Over and over again.

His story revealed the suffering he'd endured in childhood. Was the work we were meant to do, separately and together in this reuniting, about moving through our conditioned perceptions of oppression, and our assessments of our inherent worth? Was our reuniting a gift for me on my journey to awakening? Was it an opportunity for me to take personal responsibility for my actions and reactions? Was it an opportunity to recognize that I had created a false story, a myth, a reflection of my own projection?

"My partner and I are working through a separation," he informed me. I looked at him in disbelief.

"Every relationship is an opportunity for you to know yourself better, Eddie. It's not just about honor and respect externally, which is futile. It is about honoring and respecting yourself," my friend MB had said over the phone when I told her about reuniting with PJ. The raw intimacy I felt with PJ left me feeling unstable at the core. Yearning for love and loving, while honoring and respecting myself, was truly the lesson.

I stand eight degrees below the equator in front of the thick brick wall on the uneven brick steps three kilometers from Ubud center. I look toward the rustic bronze gate with the ceremonial brick temple at the compound's entrance. I am witnessing the pain once cloaked in tears shifting. I am attuning to the wisdom, vitality and peace on the island, my "home." I am protected; the unwanted demons cannot enter. I invoke the loving embrace of the magical influences, while releasing all that is not perfect.

✑

In 2005, a few years before I lived in the Potrero Hill home, my life plan had changed in an instant. A carefully paved plan had vanished into thin air. I was not prepared emotionally, physically, mentally or spiritually.

I was escorted to a small room, down a narrow hallway where framed motivational posters lined the walls. I could hear the trickle and splash of the small waterfall from the waiting area. In the room I was handed a long clipboard with layers of forms attached. On the front of each page, in 20-point red type, were the words "DO NOT PHO-TOCOPY!"

I read each sheet, soaking in the words. A question on one form asked, "What is your sexual preference?" with the choice to circle homosexual, bisexual, heterosexual, or curious.

Was I curious? Yes. Curious about life, curious about my heterosexuality, my bisexuality, my homosexuality.

"Why are you here?" asked Mark, the nurse practitioner, a thin man with short sandy hair and designer glasses. He looked over the completed forms, reading my responses and unusual answers, laughing at my humor.

His eyes showed compassion and warmth. He sensed

my nervousness, vulnerability, and shame—I was physically cloaked in layers of wool, cotton and fleece, hiding.

"How do you feel?" he asked gently.

"I feel okay," I said. "I'm a bit sluggish, it's been a long week."

"How do you spell your last name?"

"D-O-B-B-I-N-S. I'm a descendant of King Robert the First of Scotland, of the Knights Templar on one side, and African kings on the other. But you can call me by my first name, Eddie … like Oprah." We both smiled, acknowledgment of humor as my personal response to AIDS.

Dr. Marcus Conant, whom I'd seen almost three years earlier, had said, "Dear heart, it's not every day I have a patient who walks in with laryngitis, and walks out of my office with full blown AIDS." He was a gentle man whose husky southern voice resonated confidence.

My life after that became a series of numbers I did not understand. Numbers I did not want to understand.

"I am missing life," I said to Mark as tears rolled down my face, internal howling, like the virus, swirling through my body at unknown speeds and detection. I continued, unspoken truths slipping out of my mouth unrehearsed. "I miss being touched. I miss the magic of another human being's touch. I miss laughing. I miss joy. I miss being loved by another spiritual human being. I miss intimacy."

Mark listened intently as I shared my pain and my doubts that I would survive. I felt his love and concern. I felt like I had met a friend, someone with whom I could be authentic and share my truth.

He took in each word, then embraced me, an uncommon gesture in the medical profession. "Eddie," he said, giving my right earlobe a gentle pull, "you are going to live."

When I left his office that afternoon, on the road to "recovery," it was with a prescription for a new "cocktail." I would no longer be taking thirty prescribed antiretroviral medicines, which I felt had taken root in me like poison: 10 mg Lipitor, 200 mg Sustiva, Trizivir, Viread and Kaletra. I would no longer need weekly injections of chemo and applications of radiation onto each visible lesion from my feet to my shoulder blades.

When I'd first started the medication, I watched and waited for the lesions to disappear—day after day, month after month, moving through the critical stages of Kaposi sarcoma—living in embarrassment, in a self-enclosed cocoon, separated from life and myself, terrified of being seen. I often wondered if this was the punishment Mrs. Robinson had threatened me with in third grade. The fear of "coming out" to others haunted me, made me feel weak, like I was giving in to AIDS.

∽

"You are going to live" echoed in my ears as I ran home that day and began to dream. I journaled—not about my death, but about life and living. I pulled out my collection of AIDS journals and read random entries aloud, mentally letting go. Letting go of thoughts whispered from the despair known only to me.

### February 2002

My heart pounds, racing to blowing heat from the rectangular vent embedded in the wall. I am fighting with myself, and yet allowing words to just come. My mind tries to block them with reason, with logic.

Tears glisten in my eyes, like babies' teardrops floating down the sides of my cheeks. This is so difficult to write ... these thoughts lingering in my mind, coming alive.

### March 2002

San Francisco skies have turned blue this morning. The temperature has risen to eighty degrees, birds chirp. The smell of fresh brewed coffee stirs my senses, as the caffeine jolts my tongue.

Writing has become difficult, yet necessary. Today it is about facing my truth, learning how to let go of fear which has haunted me for some time.

There is a tightness in my stomach, an urge to stop writing. There is an uncertainty of what, who, why—I continue to write. Is writing a release? Is writing a way to hide behind the black ink? There is much to say; I realize it is about courage, and hope.

In less than 24 hours, the world reality you have created up to this moment will never be the same. So, as a child of God, let me ask you, what reality would you like to create—in this moment? These questions are spiritual in nature, and the answers lie in the depth of your soul's purpose.

The moment has come. Tears flow. Stomach tightens. Today—a revolving door of information and letting go of fear—learning how to participate in the consciousness of it all.

## *April 2002*

As I walked back from the corner of Divisadero and Fulton, the sun beamed from the hungry sky. The wind moved and pushed the fog over the city. The taxi I preordered was late, patience overcame me, a lightness of sorts. As I looked up, a yellow taxi pulled in front of me, from nowhere. A gift of consciousness, I thought to myself.

The driver sat quietly behind the wheel, I entered through the rear door. I noticed the driver had extended growths from his face and arms. He drove through Golden Gate Park to UCSF Medical Center. The feeling, at that moment, was calm but I knew that my world was about to take a different course, and I knew, in my soul, that I had to meet this course with strength and courage head on. Yet, I am afraid.

What is it that I fear? My hands scribble across the thin lined paper. Tears come. They are tears of letting go—tears of cleansing, tears of fear washing away.

What is it that I fear? Death?

The biggest fear in my life, in this moment, has been uncorrected and has been faced with courage and reflection. To open the door, to meet fear on the other side—there are two choices: close/slam the door, run like hell to the other side; or learn to live, walk through the open door, embrace the fear head on—notice the fear was on the other side.

## May 2002

The wick of the lit candle pokes through the melted liquid, the wick's red knit mesh creates a multitude of colors as the flame slithers toward the heavens.

The flame danced, hypnotically, music to the rhythm of the wind.

The words uttered from my lips, like a whispering child, crying out for help, for guidance.

As one is led toward the path of truth, it is the flame, the light, which returns us home. Thoughts, words and action enter the consciousness.

Thoughts of being sick craze me, like the fire from the flame.

I stir with emotions, unbalanced, scarred, and fearful of the word.

The purple dots, red with jagged edges, bracing inner thighs, like a butterfly, to a cocoon.

Inspired, Inoperable. Disguised.

I am fearful that the purple bruised dots have a name.

I am worried—but feeling strong.

I am reminded of the song, "Like a bridge over troubled water, I will lay me down." The troubled water is the angst which ravages my body, my be-ing, preventing me from breathing.

The bridge, my spirit, my partner, my guide, my foundation—I will lay me down, pray over the troubled water.

## July 2002

Tears roll down my face, like rain tapping my bedroom window. The wind howls, hails, thumps in the night, against the wooden deck—echoing, like the virus swirling through my body. I am in silence, thinking how love is present, in the midst of surviving—something I do not understand.

Evening: I understand the poetic language of words, manifesting from the lips of knees, limbs, bruised eyes; what am I to learn, here, now?

A black man scarred by the injustice of unfound freedom.

When I look at my arms, scarred by the purple lesions, unwanted tattoos, covering my body—unwelcome. I find

I am alone, home—deeply connected to the whispers of eagles calling.

I have never felt that I was ready for the world, but always wanted to take the world on—I guess this is the task at hand?

## December 2002

I am surrounded by silence. Home, quiet. My bedroom, cave, encloses the nippiness of chilled air circulating through the muffled sounds of hissing heat from the other side of the room. A numbness overcomes me. I shiver. Occasionally. Waiting. Watching. Waiting. For the moment to capture the fleeting thoughts, as I scramble for meaning.

Seven pills rest in my palm, unscathed by the purple dots on my left hand. The green fitted sheet, the texture of the pills, reflect an image of accountability.

Death is imminent.

The pills, grouped by color, remind me of the rainbow—flag. I stop.

## January 2003

The dishwasher spins in cycles,
a life pattern of sorts?
The television—the storm has not arrived
in San Francisco as promised.
This past week off (of work) has given me time
to reflect and rest.

To stop. To participate in the world differently,
authentically.
Living an authentic life in a monetary world
is a challenge.
The stress of economics overcomes me—
a fear with a twist.
I recognize this too is a gift.
Yet, I know not how to participate with it.
I find myself trying to figure out how to serve, how
to be of service.
It is a challenge I face every day, every moment.

## February 2003

"Why are you thinking of me?" the soft internal voice asked.

"I am thinking of you because you have shown me how to walk, how to laugh, how to smile, how to be patient, how to sustain in courage." How to survive? How to love myself, the whole of me.

I compassionately smile with peace and balance.

I have entered yet another sacred fraternity, one with millions of participants, participating, every day, like I do. I will survive.

## August 2003

Life Process: Begin to recognize the importance of truth: understanding and recognizing truth—living and participating in truth—are elements of manifestation, of

our individual transformation. For the individual transformation to occur, a connectivity of spirit needs to be
recognized and embraced—how do we recognize truth?
Can truth be shadowed by fear?

St. Augustine says: "I probed the hidden depths of
my soul and wrung its pitiful secrets from it, and when
I mustered them all before the eyes of my heart, a great
storm broke within me, bringing with it a great deluge
of tears ... I kept crying, How long shall I go on saying,
'tomorrow, tomorrow'? Why not now?"

## *September 2003*

Fading in and out of consciousness state—unbalanced,
but with strong heart and in identified clarity. Clarity
not in the sense of "clear" or "clearness"—unidentified
clarity, like the colors, shaped buttons, fleshed in "color
purple"—like a Seurat painting—with noticeable char-
acters—pierced on my body—permanent tattoos, inked
motionless, metamorphosis?

I have begun to name them, like the many friends who
have entered my life, revolving, in motion like a treadmill,
powered by the wind of a child's breath.

Clarity is a simple gift, like touch, faith, hope, courage—unconditional love. All intangible gifts. I fade in
and out of consciousness, unbalanced, strong heart, and
unidentified clarity.

*Guerneville, California, January 2004*
The music in my heart
echoes
in silence.
Visible scars
pain
past and present.
Quietness of surrendering
escapes me,
reality created in this moment.
I cry
inside,
alone,
with you near me.
Invisible light
beaming
resonance
of shadows call—
Am I home?

*March 2004*
The white mist of the ocean's whistling waves captures
pockets of wind, leaving its impression on my soul.

∽

## Potrero Hill – 2005

*"You're going to live."* I created a plan to live. I dreamt

big. There was no stopping me. The weight of the virus was lifting. I wrote down everything that came to me, and highlighted it in different colored ink, unlike the spotted purple lesions that dotted the surface of my skin but were now subsiding into nothingness:

*Masters—Higher Education*
*—I thrive for cutting-edge inquiry*
*Global Travel*
*Sustain Good Health*
*Financial Security*
*New Job*
*Life Partner*

I took a trip to Rio de Janeiro. Even though I felt like a changed man, the sun was drowning me, as I had worn long sleeves and long pants to hide the last of the lesions still marking my body. The temperature hovered around 100 degrees Fahrenheit, and as I walked through St. Moritz, a hilltop artist community, I began to remove layers of clothing. My shirt went first, exposing bare arms. Fear moved through me like a locomotive gaining velocity as I exposed myself. I stepped outside of fear while stepping into the fear.

I embraced in gratitude the beauty that surrounded me and the beauty of the lesions whose life was on a new course, dissolving, disappearing into the nothingness.

Accepting for the first time, embracing for the first time, exposing for the first time, all of me. I began to pray, clapping my hands in the wind, imagining a mosquito.

The funny lesson of this "coming out" on top of St. Moritz is that no one but me noticed the "marks of injustice" dotting my arms. This acceptance assisted me in shaping my plan to live, to write, to create, to delight in life.

I celebrated moments. I unclothed the brittle skin. I unleashed the barriers of sight. I opened my heart to listening. Not just listening to the singing of birds, or chimes of pipes, or buzzing of insects, or footsteps in leaves, or a cascading brook. I began to listen within. I gained a new partnership with my inner voice. I reconnected to spirits tangible and intangible. I listened to the faintest murmur through the invisible cloaked silence, a silence nurtured in hope and faith. A whisper so faint: *Live, Eddie, live. Get up and live. Run, don't walk.*

# CHAPTER 6

# I Am Centered and Meet the World with Strength and Flexibility

**San Francisco, California – 2010**

My move to Corbett Heights in 2010 marked a new beginning, a fresh start personally and professionally. An opportunity for reinvention and rekindling of the dream. I had completed a master's degree. I had secured my financial future. I created a plan for global travel, and successfully negotiated a return to the private sector after a successful public sector career. My health was on track and I was physically strong. I had the momentum to live, to love, to experience life at unimaginable levels. I felt grateful and centered. I moved forward with the intention to live with HIV.

Corbett's one-bedroom apartment allowed my wings to expand to their full breadth, catalyzing a commitment to my new life, guided by principles of tactical excellence and focused intentions. Every space offered comfort wrapped in minimalism. It was a sanctuary that provided room for growth—personally, professionally, spiritually, mentally and physically.

The apartment overlooked San Francisco, a representation of my feeling of belonging.

I was able to let go of ambivalence and the feeling of exile and rejection. On a clear day, I could see the Bay Bridge, Mount Diablo, and flights taking off from the San Francisco airport.

A Rumi quote on a magnet on my refrigerator was a reminder of my journey home:

Come, come, whoever you are,
Wanderer, worshipper, lover of leaving.
It doesn't matter.
Ours is not a caravan of despair.
Come, even if you have broken your vows a thousand times.
Come, yet again, come, come.

My daily spiritual practice deepened, through focused concentration. I experienced moving through the astral realms. Deeper mediation, contemplation, prayer and chanting—such practices supported my new life of living uncloaked. The universe was supporting me, my determination to succeed, to love, to create a life out of who I was and who I was becoming. Trust was the bridge to my inner voice. My divine intuition was strengthened. I listened with a deep ear to the ground, to the roots, to the soil, to the heart unfolding as a lotus flower.

I meditated, prayed, journaled and set intentions. I used humor to face challenging times, and called my soul to attention. Finding this refuge in daily meditation allowed me to take moments to pause and relax with eyes closed, to be with the rise and fall of my breath as it spiraled and moved throughout my body. It moved in a rhythm from the top of my head, slowly, lovingly, gently, downward—a teardrop on a window pane gravitating downward from my skull, to my forehead, touching my eyes, nipping my mouth, my tongue, piercing my teeth. Bones crackled, awakening my muscles from my jaw to my neck.

Scanning my body, I allowed images of nurturing to arise, noticing purples, blues, orange and terracotta clothed in cashmere-like softness. Alone in my sanctuary, steeping in the image, feeling open with my chest spread wide, lingering in dimples of moments, feeling free, comforted, I was safe and nurtured. Meditation was a tool for focusing inward during moments of cyclical fear.

My Corbett home allowed me to be creative, to perceive my thoughts and feelings with clarity instead of becoming entangled in them. Inner disturbances were held in love and in the light of radiant positive energy, which I directed through my seven chakras, from my crown down to my third eye, throat, heart, solar plexus, down through my tingling navel, my sacral center, to my prostate, my coccyx, through the root—my base.

The Corbett Heights neighborhood was my return to social, political and LGBT activism. "You are going to beat this" echoed in my head as I looked out my living room window at the Rainbow Flag in the distance. Confident words uttered by the first person I told I was HIV positive: "You will beat this."

"Mayor Brown is looking for a District 8 Field Organizer for his 1999 re-election campaign. Would you like to put your name in the hat for consideration?" my friend George had asked, upon my return from Italy in 1998. He didn't know about the dreams I'd had during my six months in Italy, after a year-long around-the-world spiritual journey in 1997.

"Exactly what does a District 8 Organizer do?" I asked. I'd had a short but successful career with small startups, which had brought me to the West Coast. But organizing a campaign was something I'd wanted to experience since studying Political Science in college. The message I'd dreamed in Italy, that did not make sense at the time, was: "Dear one, you will return to San Francisco to work alongside a man and a team of people." I got that job.

## 2002

"He will see you now," his personal secretary said. I got up nervously from the chair where I'd been waiting for my appointment with the Mayor of San Francisco. I climbed the marble stairs to the Executive Offices of the City and County of San Francisco. My footsteps were audible as I walked the marble floors, past offices for the Chief of Staff and the Private Secretary. I walked through the Hall of Mayors, where photographs of the city's mayors lined the walls—all white men with sad-looking faces, Senator Dianne Feinstein the exception. My heartbeat echoed in my ears.

I was escorted through thick wooden doors into the office where Mayor Willie L. Brown, Jr., sat behind his carved wooden desk. Behind him was a long credenza with photos of celebrities, his family, and my favorite—him and JFK, Jr. He graciously motioned me toward the leather chair opposite him.

"What can I do for you, Dobbins?" he asked. His clasped hands formed a teepee of loosely touching fingers. His nails were manicured, buffed, setting off his ring, which sparkled in the afternoon sun streaming through part-opened blinds. His purple silk tie was almost hidden by a buttoned up, pinstriped jacket tailored to perfectly fit his broad shoulders.

His tone was authoritative, yet familiar and respectful.

I had rehearsed, rehearsed and rehearsed this moment—every word. I knew I had to be sharp, on my toes, speak in bullet points, wrapped in a short story. He had successfully won the general election and a runoff special election, covered by many major TV news stations in the country.

The runoff election had pitted Brown, the first elected African-American Mayor of San Francisco, against Tom Ammiano, President of the Board of Supervisors, and openly gay. The battleground—District 8—included the Castro, the heart of the LGBT movement and community. Where Harvey Milk had changed the political landscape for gays nationally and internationally, and where Sylvester, the first black gay music icon, had become a star.

"Well, sir," I said, as if I had just learned a new English phrase, "I was told by London that you wanted to see me regarding a project."

"Yes." His look was laser-focused.

*How do I tell this man I cannot do a project. How do I say "No, I can't" to Willie Lewis Brown, Jr.?*

During the few seconds of my discombobulation, I marveled at his meticulous organization: every object in the room, all the furnishings and pictures, were placed with perfect symmetry, with an air of feng shui. Fire engines howled in the distance, their sirens matching what I was feeling inside.

"Sir," I said, looking straight at him. No looking away, no looking down. The truth and nothing but. His hands remained clasped, his fingertips slowly tapping together.

"I wanted you to hear it from me first." I paused. A quietness seemed to move through his office. I felt like floating away on the Oriental rug. I sat straight, back perfectly balanced, shoulders down, confident, hiding a quiet stir of guilt and embarrassment.

"Sir ... I came to tell you I have HIV/AIDS. I am in the midst of a radical treatment and my energy level is unpredictable." My voice was calm. In that moment I felt I was in a state of grace.

His body shifted. He unclasped his hands and the teepee came down. His eyes teared up as he looked into mine. I was moved by his support. I felt a peace I had never experienced in his presence. I had been on bar crawls with him, been the occasional recipient of his outbursts over the phone, engaged in private conversations with him about his car collection, even eaten ice cream with him in Noe Valley, a District 8 neighborhood. But I had never felt this kind of intimacy.

"Who is your doctor?" he asked in a fatherly tone.

"Dr. Conant," I said, knowing he and the doctor had worked together at the height of the AIDS epidemic.

"You are in great hands. He's one of the best," he said with a nod of approval. "What do you need?" he asked.

"I'm good ... now, sir." I felt a relief, the tightness unraveling. Yes, even a feeling of serenity in the large office of the sitting Mayor of San Francisco.

"If there is anything I can personally do for you, do not hesitate to let me know."

"Thank you, sir."

He stood, pushing the leather chair backward toward the credenza, the ring on his left hand reminding me of my father's. I stole another glimpse at JFK, Jr., as the Mayor came from behind his desk to stand in front of me. His strong grip encircled me, and we embraced, like father and son.

He watched as I moved through the security doors leading to the Hall of Mayors. As I pulled the handle of the door behind me, I heard ...

"Eddie" (not "Dobbins"). I turned, still holding onto the gold-plated doorknob.

"Sir?"

"You will beat this!"

∽

"You will beat this," my friend MB echoed during our discussion about moving through fear. "Missy," MB said (Missy is a nickname for me that only she uses), "in fear there is equanimity." It was one of her one-liners—a curve ball with intentions. "Fear is simply the light, the presence, a sign that you are on the path, your path," she said. "Fear means you are growing. Life is preparing you for more experience of life."

I sat with her words for a moment. "Are you saying fear is generated by the mind?"

She looked at me, her bifocals and tiny rose-colored nose a mirror of my mother and my Aunt Jane—waiting for me to process, dig deeper.

"So fear arises when there is a belief that 'it' can't be handled. The 'pain' is grounded in the belief that we are not strong enough to handle the pain!"

"You got it, Missy." She smiled and stirred the mushrooms simmering in olive oil on the stove. She scooped boiled basmati rice into the pan along with a pinch of spices. She looked at me and tossed out a Gandhi one-liner: "Where there is fear, we lose the way of our spirit."

"Missy," she said, pouring me a glass of red wine, "in the writing you have shared with me about your family distress … " She paused, as I sat patiently waiting for her schooling. "You have carried uncertainty with you, dropping a thimble of sand each time you move through a difficult situation. You, my dear one, have made it through some of the moments, as I have, through the faith you are grounded in—which is visible on your sleeves—faith pours through you. It is what gives *me* strength."

She took a sip of her white wine, an unwavering gleam

in my eyes. "Faith is a verb," she said looking directly into my eyes, watching my wheels turning.

"Faith." The word hung in thin air, motionless. "Faith is a way of being." We looked at each other, our wine glasses meeting in the air, a click, and a long quiet pause. "Faith is your spiritual practice. You move through life, consistently discovering, molding, cementing what is reliable and true. Almost like a trust in your inner wisdom, your inner voice."

She was right. She hit the nail head-on, and confirmed she was a participant in my story, as I was in hers.

Faith had been brewing inside me from the moment I entered the Universe, the world, from my mother's womb.

"Your equanimity is your ability to experience changes in your life while remaining calm, centered and unmoved. Your growth, your relationship to faith, your trust in an infinite capacity has deepened. You don't withdraw, you expand."

∽

The white popcorn ceiling, the walls and floor of my bedroom protected my body, covered in layers of cotton: sheets, blankets and comforters. The number 37 bus engine roared into gear, shifting down the hill. Rain blanketed the city, taking no prisoners.

A different roar ... the grinding sound of a truck being

forced into gear? Flapping wings ... a moose? The fault line under the foundation of 311 Corbett? Startled by the noise, now completely awake, my body jolted. Bits of white popcorn sprinkled down, landing on the comforter I was cowering under. Earthquake?

On the nightstand my iPhone vibrated to a rhythm of its own. *707 Area Code.* "Good morning?" I was still vibrating with the movement and sounds of mother earth.

"Are you rested, ready for the work later this morning?" Her voice was light, nurturing. *Catherine.* She was making sure I was prepared for our session.

"I am," I said.

"Great! Did you drink a lot of water?"

"Yes."

"No heavy foods, no tobacco or drugs."

"Nope, none of those things," I acknowledged, looking at the particles of white dust, like grains of sand, coating the comforter and rug. "I'm excited to see what will be revealed."

"Wonderful! I'll see you soon."

Swooping sounds came through the clouds, needling my senses. I stood in soaking socks on the wet balcony holding a hot glass of freshly brewed tea. The brisk smell of the black herbs jolted me to consciousness, yet an invisible thread pulled me back into the gray clouds. *Is this a dream?*

*Delia's Book: Guidance for Cancer Healing,* by Catherine Held, had compelled me to seek her out. I felt driven to experience the ancient healing techniques she details in the book, and I was already working with much of what she teaches: guided prayer, focused intention, therapeutic touch. I was also interested in seeking assistance for my mother's cancer.

When I made the appointment with Catherine, she sent me an email: "Hi Eddie, I look forward to seeing you on April 10 at 11 a.m. You have an interesting background—our session will run 1.5 hours. I suggest you reflect on your intentions for healing, as the energy work operates on many levels. Catherine."

## Darius – 2003

I met Darius, a teacher who provided inspiration and an awakening for me, over the phone in late 2003. He showed up in my life through infinite wisdom, through some mystical connection to Source. Our work together supported my path and helped me gain access to greater knowing and insight. He encouraged me to step into the "unknown," to connect to my inner peace, my unconditional loving, my clarity and purpose. He moved me to overcome the fear and self-doubt that had stuck to me since I'd been diagnosed with HIV/AIDS.

"What brings you to me?" he'd asked. His voice

reflected a love that seemed caring and poetic, a kind I had never known. As if cellos, strummed softly by angels, were playing background music over the phone.

I stuttered uncontrollably, a whining child needing to be heard, seen and given guidance. Fear wrapped itself around me, suffocating every molecule, cell, membrane in my body. He listened patiently to my unreeling. There was a long pause, then a vibrational energy, a sound wave moving through my ear, through my body.

"Eddie, I may be wrong, but this is how I see it. Your life has been on a collision course. The events of childhood and running away from who you are. Your intentions need to lie in how you remove all obstacles, barriers and fear, how you define your purpose in the world."

I listened, carefully jotting down bullet points. His insights tore at me, twisted inside of me. I was experiencing an exorcism, a curling inside, pushing from the pit of my stomach through my esophagus.

"Eddie, your steps are to create a plan for peace in your life ... and then activate it. Obstacles must be healed before you can move forward. Take the smallest steps possible to support the process ... your process. Skipping a single step is not advisable."

He heard my faint sigh, a letting go, a release of sorts.

"In order to live in the energy that we're living in today, you must stay on top of what you are feeling, you must pay attention to the recurring patterns. Eddie, please listen as I share this."

My panic button was pushed. My heart dropped to the ground, then broke through to an abyss of no return.

"You are in the world, but you are not of this world. Your evolution occurs through adverse experiences. You cannot think aware, you can only be aware."

A thunder of tears was untangling inside, unraveling, erupting. A root shifting in earth's soil.

"Eddie, I encourage you to pray. Write about your emotional honesty as a way to begin your process, your journey. My beautiful spirit, you will begin to take solace when there is accountability and responsibility for your emotional honesty. You will discover what emotional dishonesty is—what you have been holding on to for too long."

Darius hit a nerve, one tender and bruised. Thoughts and memories surfaced from all directions, leaping at me, urging me to change course. To let go of all that encumbered me, from "you are a worthless child for having a white mother," to the struggles and fear of coming out.

After speaking with Darius, I sat, stirred with thoughts, a spider caught in a web. A lit candle flickered on a silver tray and shadows danced as in a delicate breeze, surrendering to music. My heart pounded.

I opened my journal and started writing, capturing

words as they came, each syllable feeling ripped from my heart. Breathing. Surrendering to clarity. Standing inside a blown bubble and observing the disturbance through the shimmering glaze that distorted my peace. Salivating, crying the tears of a child becoming a man. Spiritual teachers and guides assisted me in understanding the mystery of coincidence while learning how to act on intuitive information.

His words framed my next steps through the doorway to the "unknown."

*"What truly, is your heart's desire?"* The question echoed through the window of wisdom. *"Pay attention ... you have been given a gift. You can see the light. Please don't doubt this. The lesson for you, my child, is the lesson of self-love."*

✌

Catherine's condominium-turned-healing center, an oasis of calm, was nestled in a grove of trees off Old Redwood Highway in Cotati, California. My intention was to experience deep healing and access greater levels of wisdom regarding my career and personal life.

Incense burned, and a dream catcher hung over the doorway. The hiss of burning incense, the wind of her hand-held feather fanned over my body in long circular strokes, put me in a trance. She chanted an unfamiliar arrangement of vowels, not Sanskrit or any language I could identify. Sounds, blending, beckoning Spirit.

A deep peace came over me, tension escaped from the tips of my toes and through the bristles of my hair. I was accessing resources wedged deep in the confines of my consciousness. Rhythmic music moved through her hand as she laid it on me, jolting, illuminating my clothed skeleton, now basking in guided prayer. The room cocooned my senses and enabled me to reach Samadhi (a peaceful state) with grace and ease. I returned from this journey with images. Pieces of the puzzle.

"How are you?" she asked, as she watched me return. Her auburn hair matched the feathers woven into the fan-like instrument she'd used.

"There is a calmness, a peace, a serenity moving inside me. It feels like tiny rapids, eddies," I smiled, "gurgling in hypnotic trance."

"What comes forward for you?" She smiled. A sweet pungent smell lingered, the aroma stimulated my blood, unleashing a flood of emotions.

I shared with Catherine the intentions I had set for the week and for our session. I shared my experience of being awakened by a Raven—the vulnerability I felt, the kind when you buckle over. I told the truth and nothing but the truth—to this stranger. I shared the importance of my Corbett apartment, of finding a sanctuary and creating a home. I told her about my mother's declining health.

I shared that I felt my blood moving through my body. I shared how I felt an unleashing, a letting go of the tight grip of AIDS. I shared my fear that I might lose both my parents at the same time. How I could not bear the thought. I shared about the shift I was seeing at the start-up where I worked. I shared that I felt my professional days there were coming to an end, and my writing was starting to move ahead full-throttle.

She listened intently, a glimmer of love in her eyes. Then she spoke: "Dearest, to experience the Raven means that something special is about to happen. The question, my dear, is how is Eddie going to respond to the synchronicity of the alchemy of the moment? The Raven is a messenger sent to you at this time. It is your guide home. It's a message guiding you to a change in consciousness. This change in consciousness will bring a new reality, a new state of wellness."

She continued, channeling a message I had heard before. "You are here ... there are things which surround you ... have influence over you and you over them. To penetrate the invisible world, Eddie, you have to love in the present, in the here and the now. To be in the present you have to control your second mind and look at the horizon."

Overcome with sacred messages, I heard the soft chime of an alarm that signaled the end of our session. We gazed into each other's eyes as she said, "Eddie, you have earned the right to see, to experience a little more of life's magic—the Raven's magic. This will provide you with the courage, the will, to carry the medicine as you enter the darkness of the world, which is the home of all that is not yet in form."

The resonance of her words swept away any angst or frustration I might have been experiencing prior to my arrival. She instructed me as I departed: "Eddie, call the Raven forward as a courier—to carry an intention, to bring forth healing energy. Bring the Raven to the light. Eddie, you are not equipped to move into another level of consciousness until you have mastered the one you are currently working with. Remember, be careful what you ask for."

⋨

Two months away from my first year anniversary at the startup and stock option rights, I returned from a seven-day business trip from the East Coast with a feeling inside my gut that a change was coming. Was it the report I'd completed before my trip, suggesting that the scalability of the channel direction was not in alignment with the Board? Upon my return to my glassed-in office, I was called to my newest boss's office. He informed me that he and twenty-six others, including me, were being "separated" from the company, effective immediately. My life shifted. *Is the Universe preparing me? Am I going home?*

Home, for me, was never defined in a traditional sense. Home was where I felt anchored in joy. Home was where my heart sat. It was a place of serenity, calmness, peace.

My mother's home did not represent a place of peace or calmness. Italy was home. Chicago was my birth home, Missouri and Arkansas my ancestral home. San Francisco was where my heart was cradled in the bosom of inner growth.

I immediately activated a new plan. Securing a consulting opportunity in the area of my expertise, I headed to the Midwest, to Missouri, to Chicago. After that, I would return to my spirit home: Italy.

That night, in a mystic abyss of consciousness, lighting bolts of information, synchronicities shooting from dimensions known and unknown, came through in my meditations. Unfamiliar words testing the agility of my anchor swished loosely across the lap of my journal. Ink flowing from the pen, gliding without leverage, a quote from Yogananda inspired my writings: "O Lord of Law, since all affairs are directly or indirectly guided by Thy will, I will bring Thy presence consciously into my mind through meditation, in order to solve the problems life has sent me … I am a spark from the Infinite. I am not flesh and bones. I am light ... In helping others to succeed, I shall find my own."

# CHAPTER 7

# With Compassion, I Open My Heart to Fully Commit

## Chicago, Illinois: Western Suburbs – March–April 2011

*What's next?* I asked myself as I took in the essence of my new surroundings. From the twin bed I could see a small porch light glowing just beyond the fenced yard of my mother's home. Dark became light, and the familiar sound of birds chirping under the maple tree outside my bedroom window brought home the undeniable fact that I was living in my mother's ranch house in the Western Suburbs.

I had never imagined returning to live in my mother's home. I'd made a vow to visit only on selected holidays and to stay no longer than a week. It usually took only twenty-four hours before nasty words and negativity took over our interactions.

"No, Eddie, you cannot drive my car while you're here," she'd said in her usual matter-of-fact way. So I'd shipped my Ford Focus to Chicago.

The one time I was allowed to drive a car registered to

my mother was shortly after I'd passed my driving test. I'd gently nudged her one Saturday evening, while she was resting from her forty-hour workweek at American National Bank and Trust in downtown Chicago. She was a self-taught accounting whiz. She said yes. I drove to visit a friend. All turned out fine, but that was the last permission I ever received.

∽

I had moved back in with my mother partly because my half sister had rejected any notion of doing so.

"I am not moving back to Chicago to take care of her," she shrieked. "I don't want that house. I've lived with her, and I do not need her to control my life. I have my life in Kentucky." Instead, she had convinced my mother that the solution was for our mother to move to Kentucky.

Mom had agreed. The plan was that I would return to Chicago for a few months to prep the house to be sold and to help her get organized for the move.

When I arrived in late March, my half sister, her daughter, and her new husband of a few months were already there. We planned to celebrate our mother's seventieth birthday on April 2.

With the demands of caring for Mom and monitoring her chemo regimen, I was sleep-deprived and exhausted by the end of the first week. I watched in pain as my mother's small body was swallowed into an abyss of man-made chemicals. Before my return, she laughed, wept and drove herself to and from injections, exhibiting strength, courage and determination in the face of death. Was this something I'd inherited?

To ground myself before bed each night, I set intentions, did a series of self-forgiveness exercises, mediated and prayed. I had long ago incorporated this daily ritual into my schedule to cope with back-to-back meetings, airplanes, airports, hotels and conventions. The habit was now in full force:

I intend to further deepen my connection to Spirit—toward my life purpose.

I intend to seek clarification and understanding of personal and family relationships, so that I may be of service.

It is my intention to send light to my family and friends who need encouragement, and to my ancestors for carving a path for me to walk.

I accept responsibility for my inner experience and take dominion over my consciousness so that I may empower myself to resolve issues and experience emotional freedom.

I intend to further explore and embrace the acceptance of what is—accepting my feelings and those of others involved.

I know that how I relate to myself while I go through

an issue, is the issue.

I intend to acknowledge myself for having the courage and willingness to take responsibility for my emotional reactions and to apply loving to the places inside where there is emotional pain.

On the morning of April 2, I darted off to Starbucks for my morning coffee, which allowed me a brief getaway before the influx of guests. As I sipped my coffee, I reviewed the past few days and our preparation for Mom's birthday. We'd gone party shopping together, which had turned into a strenuous nine-hour day. Each consumable item had passed through Mom's rigorous inspection. Expiration dates were examined and each item reviewed thoroughly for color, quality and freshness. The packaged lettuce had to be hand-inspected. Watching my mother meticulously examine each can, bottle, carton of eggs and container of milk helped me understand that she was not just being picky, but was being purposely mindful of what she ate in order to support her fragile health. I'd felt a sense of peace with that realization, which deepened further when I spied the monthly calendar on the wall in the kitchen. Mom's handwriting was in black ink in the tiny square box for April 2: I MADE IT! TIME TO CELEBRATE!

*April 2011*

There is a smell of rain, a sweetness, sprinkles of fresh-plucked herbs. The sound reminds me of a waterfall taking periodic breaks from her flow. The wind blows a burbling howl ... an image comes to mind of puffing cheeks blowing air. Mumbling metal wind chimes—a combination of the still wind and the silence of the rain from the darkened sky.

I have been in Chicago for exactly one month. The past four weeks have shown me the breadth of the word "courage." Honoring courage in yourself and other human beings is the beginning of healing. My mother was a "stacker" (an emotional trigger) in my movie, my journey. I see the movement and connectedness of the choice I made to live with her again. Whether the choice is right or wrong, the starting point is to recognize the judgment placed on the choice—if judgment is taken away from the choice, what are we left with?

Setting clear boundaries proved to be the opening of a vault that had been closed for many years. On one occasion, in the first few days of my return, we were talking. She sat at the kitchen table smoking; I was standing. At one point her words and tone triggered an electric charge in my body, knocking me out of my shoes of confidence and returning me to the little boy who was frightened, confused and alone. Black and white images of a past scenario flashed in sequence through my memory.

I saw her with a cigarette in her left hand and a thick electric coffee-pot cord tightly looped around her right wrist, the end of the cord dangling, moving. Swirling smoke belched from her cigarette. She was wearing a blue and white cotton blouse with matching shorts and white sandals, her thin brown hair rolled tight in plastic curlers. We were in the courtyard of the brick apartment building, where windows looked down from all directions. Neighbors peeked, listening. There she stood waiting, posed in her summer elegance.

"Where in the *hell* have you been?" she asked, loud as if she stood on Soldier Field's 50-yard line addressing a packed stadium. "I have been calling you for twenty minutes." Her tone rose like Jessie Norman moving up the scale in "Amazing Grace." The peering heads assembled. They knew her routine.

"At the park, Mommy," slipped from my tongue.

"You are fifteen minutes late." I watched the black cord dangling like a string on a kite waiting to take off. Her cigarette hinged, glued to her lower lip. With her left hand gripping my left wrist, she swung hard and fast, not missing a body part. The humiliation sliced into my flesh. The image of the discarded cigarette as she took it from her mouth and threw it into mid-air, like a flame shooting from an open fire pit, is forever carved into my memory.

In my mom's suburban kitchen, I stood in a state of paralysis as that memory moved through my body and I slowly returned to our discussion. My white socks felt glued to floor. In a loving voice, I asked, "So that I am clear as to what I am hearing, in your tone ... could you share with me what your 'tone' is saying?" The words slipped out like feathers, floating, fluttering as I waited, watched, waited for her reply. I asked myself, *What is the blessing here?*

She sat in silence anchored to the kitchen chair, her feet dangling. The moment seemed like an eternity. Her lit cigarette, wedged in the grooves of the glass ashtray, provided bravado as the smoke lingered like a backdrop in a Donna Summer video.

"I sometimes get agitated, not so much at you, but with what's going on around me. So my words come out in ways that sound too loud or like I might be mad. But most of the time, after my chemo treatments, I get cranky and tired. You happen to be the one who 'benefits' from these outbursts." She smiled and said lovingly, "I'm sorry."

I stared in disbelief. She was apologizing! She had taken the time to *hear* me. And I took the time to *hear* her. In that moment, I found my blessing. Her tone had "disturbed my inner peace," which triggered an old story held inside me (indicating an opportunity for healing).

The blessing of being heard and receiving the clarification I had asked for led to a positive shift in our relationship and our ability to communicate. A path forward had been cleared.

# CHAPTER 8

## Forgiveness Frees Me to Speak the Truth

**Ubud – December 12, 2011**

Three soft knocks vibrate against the wooden door. I glide across the floor, stirring the geckos on the ceiling, who slither away to hide.

"Hello, good morning," she says, smiling, her eyes hidden beneath her helmet. She looks pleased. "Are you ready?" She dangles her keys in midair.

"I'm ready! What's the plan?" Kadek hands me a helmet, and we're set for our trip to the other side of Ubud.

We zoom in and out of traffic, around dogs, other mopeds, potholes hidden under debris, and groups marching in ceremonial processions. A short ride, and we arrive at the home of Ketut Leyar, the famed medicine man from the book *Eat Pray Love* by Elizabeth Gilbert. He lives on a tiny road hidden behind the main street, surrounded by undeveloped rice fields.

I have shared with Kadek that my mother and I watched the movie version of *Eat Pray Love* several times on TV in Chicago during the 203 days I took care of her. We'd enjoyed the cinematography and music. I'd felt that the film was my mother's way of participating in my travels in Italy and India.

Kadek hands me a red octagonal plastic card with the number "1" marked on it in white ink. "Oh my goodness! Thank you!" I am bursting with excitement.

She grins. "Ketut will see you at 9 A.M. You are his first client." A palm tree sways hypnotically behind her as she stares into my eyes. Stimulated by the aromas surrounding us, we walk through the compound gate. Caged tropical parrots greet us. A woman in traditional Balinese dress directs me to the front steps of Ketut's porch.

A door opens, and on the other side stands a small man. Gurgling and spitting sounds echo from inside, strangely reminding me of my paternal grandmother and the Crisco can at her bedside to provide a receptacle for her spittle.

He slowly walks to the tiled porch where I awaited his entry. "Okay … I am very happy to meet you. Where is your country?" he asks as he moves to sit on a cushion on the rustic tile floor.

"America," I say, wondering where this is leading.

"You understand me?" he asks with concern.

"Yes, I understand. I am from California."

"Have you come here before?" He looks puzzled.

"No, this is my first time," I say, hanging on each word emanating from his lips.

"You understand me from …?"

"I understand you from the movie." We both laugh.

"My name is Ketut Leyar. Wait a moment. I show you the book." He leaves the room and returns with a book. "Very old book. Elizabeth Gilbert give me the book."

He shows me the inscription: "Ketut, my teacher and friend."

"I cannot speak English very well. My name is Ketut Leyar because someone said, Ketut is very handsome. And I am very ugly. Kidding, kidding." I sense he is thrilled that an American has arrived. A letter appears from underneath the mat he is sitting on.

"Elizabeth Gilbert send me a letter. Please read it to me."

"Dear Ketut, I heard that you were sick, now I hear that you are better. I hope you can hear my prayers for you and feel my love." I mime the meaning of love and prayer with hand gestures.

"Please read again," he says in delight. I reread the note slowly so he can understand the love he is receiving from America, from Elizabeth Gilbert, who shared with the world the gift she received during her time in Bali.

"I got sick. Kidney stones." He chuckles.

I repeat, "'Now, I hear that you are better.' She is sending you prayers."

"I think of you every day," I continued. "I am grateful

(happy) for all that you taught me about love. I send you my heart."

Ketut looks perplexed. In a monotone, articulating each word, he asks, "She in love with me?" His face stretches in confusion. "Elizabeth Gilbert is very pretty. 'I send you my heart.' What is this meaning? She in love with me? Not my cup of tea. I am very ugly."

I make the symbol of love by bringing my hands together in the shape of a heart. "Love is heart," I say.

"I understand." He nods in appreciation.

"Can I take a picture of that?" I ask, pointing to the note from Gilbert.

After I take the photo, Ketut reaches for my right palm and holds it lovingly. His index finger glides across my palm. His uncut fingernail guides me to similar strokes, many years ago, at a hotel in Florence, on the morning of October 3, 1997.

∿

I had lived in Florence for part of the year in 1997. One evening, after having gone to bed, I decided to get up and walk to the Piccolo Café near Piazza Santa Croce. An intuitive voice had roused me and encouraged me to venture out to experience the nightlife of Florence.

At the café I met a Norwegian couple. A curiosity, a draw of energy, had pulled me toward their table. As I approached them—a very blonde woman and a blue-eyed man—the woman asked in English, "What brings you to Florence?" She sounded as if she already knew the answer.

I replied without irony, "I was told in a dream that I would travel around the world in search of God's existence. I was told that on this journey I would meet significant guides who would appear when called. I was told that all I had to do was pay attention." I took a sip from the beer I'd bought at the bar on my way in, and awaited their reaction. They seemed unfazed.

The woman introduced herself as Helge. She leaned toward me and whispered over the music playing in the background, "We are here to heal the monetary system of Florence." She said this without batting an eye. I sat down on the empty stool at their table.

Jarle, the man, looked at me with inquisitive eyes and chimed in. "We stayed in Florence to meet you, Eddie."

"Does this frighten you?" the women asked.

"How does one heal the monetary system?" I asked.

"We use Reiki energy," she said.

"What is Reiki energy?"

"It's energy that comes directly from your higher power, from Source. It is a system that was taught to Jesus and Buddha thousands of years ago. Before World War II, a Japanese man, Dr. Usui, rediscovered it. His spiritual quest took him to many of the places you intend to travel," the man said, without knowing my travel schedule included India and Katmandu.

"He discovered an ancient recording or transcript about Reiki energy and began treating himself and later treating the poor and the homeless. You lay your hands on the body in specific formations that transmit unconditional love."

"We humans are capable of great wonders," Helge said. "With Reiki, there is a vibration, a frequency of energy raised through the 'ki,' through the opening of your chakras, and drawn through the channel." She paused. "Reiki is never sent, Eddie. The energy enters your crown chakra, then passes through your heart, your solar plexus, arms, hands, through your whole body."

The following morning I was sitting in the Hotel Medici, in a tiny room with three twin beds positioned neatly around the perimeter of the room. Each bed was made to perfection with simple cotton sheets that matched the powder blue trim on the lace curtains flowing from fifteen-foot-high windows. Photographs of the Duomo and the statue of David hung on the old Tuscan walls. The shutters and windows were closed and locked. The curtains were closed. The door was bolted from the inside, a bronze key dangling from the doorknob. There was nothing but stillness in the room.

"Are you nervous?" Jarle asked. I was sitting on a

wooden chair in the middle of the room. I laughed like a schoolboy excitedly waiting for what would come next.

"What I am about to do is open your energy. I will be placing my hands near certain parts of your body. You might feel many different emotions. I will walk around you as you sit in the chair. Just relax," he said quietly. I sensed his concentration and love. "Are you ready?"

"Yes," I said without pause. *When the student is ready, the master will appear.*

The initiation began. Helge sat on one of the other beds. A Do Not Disturb sign had been placed on the outside of the door. If there had ever been a point to turn back, I had missed the opportunity. I could hear my mother in the back of my mind: *You went into a hotel room with two people you met briefly the night before so you could be healed by special energy? Have you lost your mind, child?*

I felt no fear. No gurgles in the pit of my stomach. I knew the Universe had brought the two Norwegians to meet me. Synchronicity. Serendipity. I was ready for the responsibility and the gift, not knowing how the gift would shape my life. I sat, feet firm on the Oriental carpet. I felt my socks tighten around my toes.

I closed my eyes, and my breathing became rhythmic, soft, pronounced. A gargle sound appeared and disappeared like the contents of a sink dissolving down a drain. I felt my heartbeat slow. The temperature of the room shifted from a damp cold to warm. Sometime later, I returned to the "present." Jarle was sitting in front of me with his legs crossed and his head bent slightly toward the floor. I had been "under" or "away" for what seemed like a week.

"How do you feel?" he asked, his pleasant tone tinged with a slight concern.

My response took time, as I attempted to put the experience together like pieces of a puzzle, trying to detect any physical changes other than the tears flowing from my eyes. I felt like a child experiencing great joy for the first time. It seemed I had traveled a far distance, to a place with no name, no description, physical or otherwise.

"I feel totally relaxed," I said, examining the perspiration in my palms.

"Did you see or feel anything?" Jarle gazed lovingly into my eyes.

"I saw two images. Two faces. One was an elderly bald man. The other was looking down, with his hands stretched out. There was light around his upper torso. The two images appeared separately and then later, together. Both with separate messages."

"You've experienced what is called the Christ Plane. There are six planes one can cross into, and each will get you to different levels of God, Christ, Buddha. You may use whatever word you like." He paused to look at Helge, who was lighting a cigarette and focused on every word. He continued. "The level some people are at is the Me level, followed by the Christ Plane level, followed by the I Am level." He stood up, brushed his hands on his jeans and opened a bottle of water. Sweat ran down the side of his neck.

"My dear one," he said, "what you have just experienced is the first half of the initiation. I have opened your energy field—to initiate you—attuning your heart and thymus on the etheric level, to prepare you to teach. This is a special gift."

He pulled on his loafers, laughed and gestured that it was time for lunch. "Lunch, lunch, lunch is on me!" he said.

After enjoying fresh Tuscan pomodoro and penne bolognaise, we visited the Medici Palace, where we recognized a past life we had shared. Jarle told me that the second part of the initiation would affect energy at the thyroid, pituitary and pineal glands, opening the throat, crown chakra, and third eye—the center of higher conscious and intuition. Sealing the channel opening as the final attunement would take place that afternoon. He would later explain that initiation typically was a two-day process, but because of time and fate and my energy field, one day would be sufficient.

In the afternoon we resumed our positions in the hotel

room. Jarle touched specific areas of my body as he whispered affirmations and chanted with closed eyes. He began with my eyes: "I see clearly with the light from within." My temples: "I balance my openness to the Universe." Back of the head: "I synthesize all of my resources for focus and creative expression." My cheeks: "Forgiveness frees me to speak the truth." My throat: "I am grateful for all the beauty around me." My heart: "I rejoice that we are truly all one." My solar plexus: "I easily give birth to my divine will." The lower level of my crotch: "With freedom I surrender to my perfection." My neck: "I am centered and meet the world with strength and flexibility." My back: "With compassion I open my heart to fully communicate." Kidneys: "I release everything that is not of perfect peace." Tailbone: "I transform all that is illusion with the infinite power of love." Lastly, he touched my feet, and heat pushed from his palms: "My understanding is perfect."

✖

Holding my right palm, Ketut looks up. "You are very, very handsome," he quivers, with a hearty chuckle. Kadek smiles, looking on.

"You already married?" he asks. He moves his hands across my body like a magician waving a wand. I wonder what he will pick up.

"I'm not," I say.

"Why?"

I look blankly at him.

"I married two time," Ketut shares. We laugh and I think of my father's twelve marriages.

Ketut continues. "You are a very good man ... good boy ... I am very happy to discuss with you ... I see your nose is very good. I see your head is very good. You are an influencer—when you talk with someone, they listen. I hope you soon marry."

He looks sternly into my eyes. "When you marry, you come back to Bali and stay in my house. Okay? I see your cheeks, left, right ... make me happy to tell you, don't worry ... very, very handsome. Don't cry, don't cry. I see your eyes, left, right ... I see married eyes ... I see happy eyes. You have one, two lines ... very, very happy to see you ... very lucky. You like king."

He chuckles. "Oh! I see you will be success ... you will be rich. Don't forget me ... I see with you. If I lie, my soul goes to hell!" He quivers with spirits surrounding him.

"What's your name?" he asks as he turns me around so my back is facing him.

"Eddie," I say, wondering *What kind of medicine man is he?* He checks my back, like a doctor in an examining room.

"You are very balanced." He looks further—an examination I have never experienced before. "Okay, okay, okayyyy! You will be one hundred years old. I am not joking. If I joke, my soul will go to hell." He examines my head line. "Very clever. Very smart."

"I have a Balinese medical book. I'll check you. You are very, very lucky! Okayyyyyy. You have heart line, but you impatient. What you do is quick, quick. I learning in English a lot from the book. I not good English ... Life line, money line, heart line. You can do many jobs. What you do you will be success. Are you writing now?"

Kadek and I look at each other.

"I am writing a book about death and dying."

"What is the name?"

*"Tea with Mom."*

"You writing, you publish your book ... You can choose one by one ... Whatever you do you will be successful. Okayyyyy ... I am very happy to tell you ... I will check the other life lines. Do publish! Business! What you do?"

"I have been taking care of my mother."

"Do your father die? Oh ... your father still alive. He good. Yes, eighty-five." He stumbles in confusion over this detail. Is there something he does not want to share?

"Now I'll check your back. You are bald there! I see there in the back a lotus flower ... You have lots of flowers in the back. Lotus flowers. You have very strong energy ... Don't worry, you will marry soon if you want. The right knee, the left knee ... no arthritis. You will be success! Okay. Very happy to me, now I give you my business card. You are a good friend."

Ketut presents me with his laser-printed card. "Namaste," he says. "See you later, alligator."

"In a while, crocodile," I say, chuckling.

A Russian tourist listening from the porch says, "Good luck on the book."

"*Dasvidaniya*," I say, accessing my limited recall of the Russian I'd memorized on a flight to the Communist country when I was fifteen. The All God's Children Choir was on a goodwill tour, through the Community Renewal Society of Chicago's cultural exchange and education through music. It was my first international flight, in 1978, before entering Oak Park and River Forest High School.

After our goodbyes to Ketut, Kadek and I move slowly through the grounds of the compound, taking in the sweet aroma of lavender and jasmine, and the clicking and musical tones of the caged parrots. We admire the small gallery of paintings and wooden sculptures Ketut has created.

Our moped ride home seems slower. The intensity of traffic, the blaring horns and screeching tires, all fluctuate in rhythm as background music. Our moped swirls in and out of the stop and go traffic. Kadek drops me off in Ubud center, where we embrace warmly and say goodbye.

"I hope you liked," she says.

"I did very much," I say. I take my backpack and head to the Art Kaffee to journal. As I walk into the Kaffee, I hear words: *Eddie, your journey has brought you here so that you may explore the deepening of your life experiences through your writing. Be patient and share your story. It will help many people.*

I recalled a mother and son bonding moment that happened during the 203 days, late one June evening when the temperatures had hit an all-time high.

I had turned the garage into a cozy sitting area, a place where Mom and I could be together and enjoy the outside world yet avoid direct sunlight on her pale withering skin.

She joined me in the garage one afternoon after napping. We sat on green folding chairs, holding hands as she listened to me read a poem by Langston Hughes, entitled "Mother to Son."

Tears began to well in my eyes as I read, each word melting away the pain of the mother's journey in the poem.

A tender moment occurred as Mom listened. Her hand in my hand brought forward an energy which enveloped us and deepened our bond. In that silent embrace I knew we were on a path of forgiveness.

Son: "What did grandmother say when she found out about the marriage?"

Mother: "She did not approve; she was very upset. I think a part of her is still upset today. She seemed to have coped with the marriage over time. She really did not make any comments until she found out I was pregnant. She wanted to know where I would go. She did not want anything black in her house. She wanted to know how I was going to 'fit' or adjust to society. I believe my mother believed that people were going to throw stones at us."

Son: "Were you scared?"

Mother: "No, I wasn't going to let society run my life."

Son: "What did grandmother say when I was born?"

Mother: "Really nothing—she made herself scarce. She did not come around or call, nor did my brother or sisters, except for the youngest. She called until she got married. Her husband didn't want her to be involved in black neighborhoods."

Son: "Where did you live when I was born?"

Mother: "Seventy-seventh at Union, which is the southwest side of Chicago, and at the time, a mixed community."

Son: "What was your work situation or environment like?"

Mother: "What people didn't know wouldn't hurt me.

I worked for a company with the responsibility of hiring and firing people. I was told not to hire niggers. All I could do was bite my lip. If I'd spoken up, my job would have been deleted. I couldn't afford that in those days, because jobs were scarce."

Son: "How did you cope with such prejudice?"

Mother: "I tried to ignore it, I pushed it aside. There was always tomorrow and every day would bring about changes. I always made it a point to keep my children in a mixed environment because I felt it would give both of you a better opportunity to get to know what people were really like."

Son: "How do you see me?"

Mother: "I see you as someone who can look at both sides and deal with life and its problems and turn them into advantages, while making things better for people who are around you."

⋘

When I was six, one evening when it seemed like midnight, my mom was sitting on the floor talking loudly on the phone to my father. She did not notice me as she began to cry (one of the few times I saw her shed a tear). She and my father had gotten into a terrible argument about money.

When she saw me, she screamed at me, then threw the

phone down and ran toward me and shook me as if I were the one on the phone. In some respects, maybe I was.

She had a bottle of aspirin in her hand, and she forced some pills into my mouth, and she took some, too. Not knowing what was going on, I became scared and threw up the pills on her white pajamas. She seemed to have been in a trance. When I vomited I guess she realized what she was doing and backed off.

I did not realize until years later that she was trying to hurt herself and me in order to get back at my father. I have often thought about that cold winter night and sometimes feel the pain of the aspirins going down my throat, like broken pebbles. Soon after that midnight terror, she enrolled me in a Catholic Sunday school. She said it was important for me to have some religious training.

As a child I lived in fear of my mother's moods. I was punished for things not grounded in reality. I felt in danger of being hurt—by my mother's love.

"How dare you love your father more than me? He has done nothing for you," she would shriek when she felt the world coming down on her. During many of her self-described "fits of anger" she would bellow, "If you don't like it here, why don't you just pack your shit and get out?" I heard this more times than I can remember.

The fear and the feeling of not belonging led me to cultivate an ability to go far away—mentally and emotionally—to a secret place where I felt less likely to get hurt.

The underlying misinterpretation of reality I bought into was that I was unloved, unlovable and unwanted by my mother. Over time, I was able to reframe my limiting interpretation of reality and see my own loving essence and my mother's as well. Shifting my perspective or "story" provided me an opportunity to heal the core of the story.

Once again I recalled the words: "Your journey has brought you here, so that you may explore the deepening of your life experiences through your writing. Be patient and share your story. It will help many people."

Opening my heart to Ketut's words, I imagined the final dialogue I wish I might have had with my mother:

Son: "Did you ever love me?"

Mother: "With all of my heart."

Son: "Why?"

Mother: "Why what, son?"

Son: "Why the abuse, the public humiliation? Why? Most of the abuse began in Chicago when I was five."

Mother: "My son, from what you are sharing, it seems like you have deep feelings about this experience. Would you be willing to share with me from your heart? You have my support and full encouragement. I sense how important this is for you."

Son: (Tears well up. The birds get louder, the wind blows, reminding me that I am safe.) "The Chicago apartment was the beginning of my awareness of the physical abuse, my first memory. In the bathroom, I had found the Johnson's Baby Powder. As I sat covered in white baby powder, you peeked in the bathroom. My laughter stopped and my smile shifted to reflect the look on your face. The look, Mom, was terrifying. You hit me with your bare hands, and I clearly remember the phrase you used that day, which became a mantra throughout most of my young life: 'I love you, but I don't like you.' So when you say, 'I love you with all of my heart,' it is so confusing and does not carry a lot of weight."

Mother: "I hear you, son. How confusing my actions must have been for you. There are no excuses, there are none. You have been the love of my life."

Son: (Laughing inside.) "I am not hearing anything you are saying. I have no desire to continue this process with you."

Mother: "Son, I know this must be difficult for you; you have my full loving support."

Son: (Silence.) "Thanks, Mom. I want to feel something more than anger when I hear you try to be nice to me. I am so confused by how you can be happy one day, and the next day, and within just a matter of minutes, you completely change into a very unloving person."

Mother: (Listening from the heart.)

Son: "I want to believe that I am the apple of your eye."

Mother: "What would it take for you to believe?"

Son: "It would be helpful if you were more consistent with your love. Talk to me in a way that is respectful and not so frightening. Show me tenderly that I *am* the apple of your eye. Change your tone. I am not my father and I am not the man of the house. I am just Eddie, looking to be loved and cared for, to be happy."

Mother: "I really hear you, son."

Son: "Thank you, Mom."

Mother: "With all of my heart."

Son: "I am afraid."

Mother: "What are you afraid of, son?"

Son: "Whenever I spoke up, it seemed as though I was punished. I was just a kid. I tried to do everything right by you. I learned very early how to find substitute love in order to protect myself from your emotional disturbance."

Mother: "What is substitute love?"

Son: "Finding love or what I thought at that early age to be love. For me it was a feeling of being protected, feeling safe. I never felt safe or protected in your company."

Mother: "Can you describe that feeling, son?"

Son: "A feeling of belonging. The feeling of being touched through respected boundaries and affection. Free to be emotionally vulnerable."

Mother: "I hear you son, so beautifully. Son, you were my firstborn. My first child. There weren't classes available on single parenting at the time. Nor were there brochures on raising a black child as a white woman. I was alone most of my life, even as a child; we are very similar that way. You immersed yourself in books to survive. I just tried to survive.

"The greatest gift through all our trials and tribulations has been getting to know myself through you. Your free will was contagious—you were and are a loving child. You are so much like me in that way. I gave birth to you in 1964 at the age of twenty-three. The year 1964 was the height of that transformational time. To give birth to you was a blessing. It was your time."

Son: (Tears. Cheeks softening, stomach yearning.) "It was my time?"

Mother: "Yes. It was your time. Or, 'I' was your time."

Son: (Puzzled look.)

Mother: "Son, you taught me so much. I was not planning on having a child. I was twenty-three, looking to find myself in the world. My mother could not show me; my father was not around. I had four siblings. My mother was a single parent, just like I would become. I protected you the best way I knew how, by giving you something I could not give myself—stability. I really hear you when you speak of the physical and emotional abuse. I am deeply saddened that this was part of your experience, your personal story and the memory of your childhood. My son, I love you so much. I created experiences that I thought would protect us as a family. It wasn't perfect but it was what I had to choose from. Yes, there were moments when I got physical with you. The orphanage was a temporary situation. It was never meant to be permanent. It was the only choice I had at the time."

Son: "The only choice?"

Mother: "I had two beautiful mixed-race children out of wedlock. I was white, young, with no job, no career—only a dream. I have no regrets. I did my best trying to support the three of us. We were barely making it most of the time."

Son: "What about the physical abuse, Mom? After we left the orphanage."

Mother: "I really hear you, son. I take full responsibility."

Son: (Soft tears. Silence.)

Mother: "I surrounded myself with people, friends who stepped up to assist me, to get me on my feet. It was not easy."

Son: "Do you ever think, Mom, that it was a bit much?"

Mother: "Yes, it was a bit much, son."

Son: (Silence. Tears.)

Mother: (Tears.)

Son: (Embracing Mom.) "All I ever wanted to feel was that there was some connection, and that I was in a stable emotional environment. As I look back at the past, the abuse was so unnecessary. The emotional bullshit phase after the beating—'I love you, but don't like you'—fucked me up."

Mother: "I really hear you, son."

Son: "It wasn't until recently that I remembered the beatings I got from your male companion. He pushed me, kicked me and hit me as I lay on the floor. The hall rug runner was squished like an accordion at my feet from my effort to find shelter from the blows. I lay there on the floor, and you stood at the end of the hall, cigarette in hand, watching the blood from my mouth and nose, smoking and just watching. One kick into my abdomen with your friend's patent leather Florsheims caught my body like a hook in the gill of a fish. You watched, cigarette smoke blowing. Why?"

Mother: "Listening to what you've shared, I sense that you're feeling hurt in response to this. Is that what you're experiencing?"

Son: (More tears.) "You think? You just stood there. Don't you think there is some feeling of hurt? (Pause.) I could take your whippings with the coffee-pot cord, with the 'I love you, but ... But you just standing and watching your friend do what he did is so hard to fathom."

Mother: (Tears.) "I hear you, son."

Son: "I was nine. Just a little boy. (Tears, gasping for air.) I did not deserve such abuse. Especially not for creating a camping scene with my GI Joe dolls in the hallway instead of going to sleep. What comes to me is that the story had to do with money. Mom, when you could not hit me anymore, is when your reckless emotional behavior began. Money was the carrot for your love."

Mother: "Money was so scarce. If you only knew what I did to have a meal on the table, to clothe you. I just wanted to show you love."

Son: "I am not the abuse. I am not the pain from the past. I do not deny that as a child I was physically and emotionally abused. As I forgive myself for the judgments I have held, I forgive you with all of my heart."

Mother: (Silent whisper.) "I am so sorry for the experience of the abuse. I ask God's forgiveness and ask for yours here and now."

Son: "I forgive you. I know you did the very best you could do at the time. Mom, although the echoes of the pain still exist, I lovingly acknowledge the times we played and wrestled on the dining room floor. I am setting the intention to hear you and participate at an authentic level—from a place of peace. Mom, I see your loving essence and understand that as I move forward into connection with Spirit, I am guided into the awareness that all is good. I am able to recognize that I am not a victim. I embrace all that has happened while continuing to move forward in the further expansion of who I am. I forgive myself for judging my childhood as unstable. The truth is that my childhood has served me well. I am fully aware of Spirit's guidance. I forgive myself for judging you as not protecting me and for holding onto the belief that I was not protected by you. I forgive myself for labeling myself as joy-*less*, for the truth of the matter is that I am joyful. I forgive myself for judging myself a victim. The truth is that I am not a victim of abuse—physical or emotional—but a recipient of courage, strength, vitality, love, compassion, kindness, humor, spontaneity and beauty!

"I forgive myself for believing that I was passed over by God."

# CHAPTER 9

# I Transfer All That Is Illusion with the Infinite Power of Love

## June 2011

One night after the Wheel of Fortune and then dinner at six-thirty—our weekday routine—my mother said, out of the blue, "I wish I could fix things between my sisters and me. I want them to know how much I love them, before I die." I later learned that at the end of life people move through a process similar to that of a 12-step program. They feel the need to make amends. For my mom, the "redress," a word I have come to embrace, was not so much about fixing anything she'd done wrong, but more about letting go of old stories that no longer served her.

Soon after she expressed her desire, I helped create the opportunity for this closure and forgiveness with her sisters. We hosted a dinner party. As we dined on pot roast, garlic mashed potatoes, vegetables and apple pie, I got to witness the laughter, stories, disagreements and apologies among the three sisters. It was like a miracle to see them in the back yard at the green garden table, sharing their love for each other, creating a new story. It was a testament to the possibility of healing and forgiveness.

One sister, Mary, whispered in my ear, "I love *this* Rita. She's so calm, so peaceful, such a joy to be around."

Mom told me later how much she enjoyed being with her sisters and that she knew her time was nearing. Thanks to the party, she was able to let go of the old stories about what her sisters had or hadn't done, which gave her a tremendous sense of peace.

This experience with her sisters spurred my mother on to continue deepening her healing in other relationships. She overheard a phone conversation I had with my cousin Mark about traveling to Missouri to visit my father, who was turning eighty-five on October 14, and she asked if she could go. I ignored her question at first; I thought she was kidding. She and Dad had not seen each other in over ten years, and it was just as well: the two of them in a room at the same time was a recipe for disaster.

She brought up the subject again, and I told her it was a great idea. I saw opportunity to bring closure to another old story she had lived with for years. It would also be an opportunity for my parents to have one last moment together. "Papa Was a Rolling Stone," by the Temptations, perfectly described the message I'd received about my father from my mother, growing up: "All he left us was alone."

As I packed the car for the road trip, I said, "Mom, whatever happened in the past, happened. It's all okay." She faced me, her hair perfectly coiffed above her perfectly assembled outfit, and peered at me through her Bette Davis sunglasses. "Can I bring up his outstanding alimony checks?"

We laughed then, but later, on the road and after some thought, I told her "no," knowing full well she had calculated the amount to the penny with interest.

Seeing my father and mother in the same physical space—embracing one another, laughing, eating, sharing, letting go of the old stories, was a magical moment. I watched as they bonded, laughed and expressed gratitude for each other. Witnessing their connection allowed me to finally honor their love story. I was awakened also to the fact that it was their love story, not mine. I was a thread in their story, but just that: a thread. Their story produced me, and in producing me, they gave me the possibility of creating my own threads with which to weave my own story.

# CHAPTER 10

# I Easily Give Birth to the Divine Within

## August 2011

My relationship with my mother deepened during a spontaneous road trip to Louisville, Kentucky, to surprise her daughter for her birthday. Driving on the open highway, past windmills, green pastures and farm fields—the backdrop of "America's Heartland"—we spoke of spirituality, which paved the way for an exchange of intimate questions.

I had created a sacred space in my Ford Focus to provide comfort for my mom. Gray, white and black feathers decorated the car's interior, incense burned, light jazz played, and the air conditioning kept us feeling refreshed. The questions and their unwinding answers showed me more of the woman, the mother, I had never known. We were like two kids discovering something new. The frankness of my mother's responses indicated she had spent time thinking about the state of her be-*ing*.

People I've spoken with in the U.S. are generally uncomfortable talking about death or dying—until it's too late. I have had very few conversations with them on this topic. In my travels throughout Europe, Asia and South America, the discussion of death and dying is embraced and respected.

"Eddie, why are you pulling over?" Mom asked. Several hours into the drive, I had noticed her hands, arms and legs twitching uncontrollably. A round of chemotherapy had been injected into her body less than ten hours earlier, and I was watching for signs of discomfort. She knew it would take a toll on her body, but she was determined to see the new home she had helped purchase. And I was determined to get her there. I just didn't know if she could survive the drive, the heat and being in that home for even a weekend.

"Need to take a stretch, Mom." I purchased a straw hat to protect her scalp from the sun. Her decline was visible in the thinning of skin on her hands, and in the puffiness of her pale white skin. Her legs, although clothed, showed diminished muscles and strength. Her clothes hung loosely on her frame. The chemo moved like the Nile through her veins, and her mood ebbed and flowed as the poisonous fluids took over her body.

"Do you pray?" I asked, back on the road after our pit stop.

Mom's hands clasped a plastic water bottle; a long bent straw made sipping easier. Her painted lips had already tattooed the tip of the straw, and as it swiveled away from her reach, she puckered her lips to grab hold. She considered her reply. "Eddie, I have prayed all my life," she answered proudly.

"Really," I responded, gripping the steering wheel with deliberate focus. I was amazed she was participating. "I can't remember ever seeing you pray."

"Just because you've never seen me, doesn't mean I don't," she said, lighting a cigarette. She took a draw and opened the passenger window. "I prayed this morning, I prayed last night." Her right foot tapped to an unrecognized beat from the radio.

The Balinese incense masqueraded the smell of the cigarette, while lightening the mood.

"What did you pray for this morning?"

Her voice cracked. "I prayed that I would last this trip. I prayed I would make it to Louisville."

A sharp sensation moved from my foot to the crown of my head. My eyes began to glisten. Her delicate fragility belied her "I will make it!" attitude.

"How do you pray, Mom?"

Her face contorted with confusion, a familiar look from the past—agitation brought on by unnecessary questions, an invasion of space.

"How do *you* pray?" She quivered slightly as she asked.

"Sometimes I pray in bed, morning and night. I

meditate so that I will hear with clarity the answers to my prayer. I pray on my knees. I pray … from my loving."

"Me too," she said. "Prayer for me is my time with God, no one else but me and my God." The cigarette sizzled as it disappeared into the water bottle.

The words "my God" rattled inside me like an uncontrollable snake, slithering, sliding. "My God" had slipped from her mouth easily, without justification or hesitation, a solid confirmation of her connection to something greater than her, a connection I was not aware that she had. The many times I'd tried to initiate conversation with her about religion, God or spirituality had been met with resistance. She seemed to have been angry with God, when in fact her anger was really directed at the Catholic Church. Her God, her prayers, were hers and only hers.

I was surprised and thrilled by the comfort my mother exhibited in sharing her thoughts with me. I learned that in spite of her anger toward the Church, she wanted to have a Catholic service and cremation, and her ashes spread in as many places as possible. She wanted to spread her wings. I told her about the Balinese cremation ceremony, in which the burning of the dead symbolizes the liberation of the soul. She loved that idea, and asked me to scatter her ashes on the island if I returned to Bali.

We arrived in Louisville in good condition, considering her frailty. Surely the conversation had lifted her spirits. But after twenty-four hours Mom was ready to return home.

"Eddie," she said. She began to cry, and then whispered, "I sat in the dark all night, and you are the only one who came to check up on me. I cannot be here. I would die in a week. I want to go home."

## September 2011

My mom and I were waiting for the doctor to enter the tiny medical office. I knew I was not fully prepared for this next step, but I also knew that Spirit was with us. The doctor lovingly told my mother that treatment options had expired and that "we" needed to be prepared to enter palliative care, followed by hospice. I knew what was happening with my mother; still, I was unprepared to hear that the end was near. I left the examining room to be alone for a moment in the hallway. I needed to cry and I didn't want to do it in front of my mother.

My mother's comprehension of the events in that small white room did not fully register. Staring out the window on our drive home, gazing blankly at the passing strip malls, she asked, "Do you think I should try another round of chemo?" She paused. "I want to be here for your birthday." My birthday is in January. She was showing her strength, just as she had all my life. She placed her left hand on my leg as I held back tears. The bellowing of tribal cries quietly stirred, tightening my muscles and intestines. My navel twitched and tightened like a coil.

Later that afternoon I scheduled the palliative care intake. The doctors had explained the difference between palliative and hospice care. I learned that hospice provides palliative care, which is a method of administering comfort and is introduced at the earlier stages of end of life care and managing pain. Palliative care is offered in many settings, including outpatient facilities, hospitals, nursing homes, hospice centers and private homes.

Our conversation during the intake centered on opening a discussion about end of life care. An hour into the intake process, it was decided my mother would go directly into hospice care. She was dying. Caring for her at this point was not solely about managing pain, but about managing time as well.

The external hospice care team provided me and her with 24-hour access to physicians, nurses, social workers and spiritual counselors. The hospice team taught me to watch for physical symptoms like shortness of breath, nausea, vomiting, constipation, diarrhea, confusion, delirium and angst. Through this observation, I was instructed on how to manage my mother's symptoms and pain. The overall care was tailored to assist my mom with specific needs as she moved through her process of dying, and as I moved through my process of feeling.

The first few days after Mom received her adjustable hospital bed, she was finally able to sleep through the night. Our mantra was "pain management." It became the focal point of our conversation each morning.

Surprisingly, a new level of communication opened up one morning after we'd had our Lipton tea. Mom acknowledged me by saying, "Eddie, thank you for caring for me. I don't know where I would be without you. I'm so glad you're here. I really did not want to go to Kentucky. I didn't know how I was going to make it through my final days financially. I could not do this without you. Thank you."

*September 2011*

The quietness of the evening reminds me of a place I cannot remember being. Watching her snore from the blue chair, I wonder: Can you teach someone to love?

As a spiritual being having a human experience, I know that God, Higher Power is in my life. I acknowledge an alignment with the light of the Universe. An energy field of love. The sounds of her breathing from her open mouth, gasping for air, nudge me to embrace the preciousness of life—but most importantly—the loving.

Can you teach someone to love? Yes! Before this moment, I would have provided a philosophical response—but now—Yes! Yes! The rise and fall of her tiny chest, covered by her long-sleeved sweatshirt …

# CHAPTER 11

# I Release Everything That Is Not Perfect

**October 2011**

After only a few hours of sleep, I woke up on the beige couch in the den, next to my mother's hospital bed. The muffled sounds of her breathing deepened. The fragrance of fresh flowers scented the room. The aroma and the vibrant color of the flowers brought calm and beauty to an otherwise grim setting. Delicate wind chimes tinkled in the breeze seeping through the patio door. The gurgles from her stomach burbled in unison to my mother's breathing—condensed, shallow and hollow—as she slept, visibly in pain.

I sat on the seat of Mom's stationary walker after administering her liquid morphine, specially delivered with required signatures. I sat quietly next to her bed, my legs dangling from the cushioned seat, my hands folded and rested in one another. I'd lit jasmine incense from Bali—Island of the Gods—that emitted a perfume of peace and stillness as the faint smoke floated through the air.

The silent sound of Om I tuned into penetrated my

body, vibrating toward my mother and connecting us through silent waves of energy. I felt her inside, on my skin, in my breath. As I centered in the silence of my meditation, I felt Spirit's light rise inside me. I could see and feel the full cycle of life, and my mother's process in her transitioning. Tears brushed my cheeks as the energy shifted in the room and within me. The tips of my fingers, to the balls of my feet, felt alive, an electric current of life moving. My heart opened, like the bloom of a lotus, expanding, awakening, growing.

I sat on the blue recliner looking out the horizontal blinds—drinking my tea alone, knowing that my tea with mom was almost over. I began making phone calls to relatives to let them know Mom was close to her transition. The first call I made was to her sister in South Carolina, a regular phone support for me. She asked me to place the phone next to Mom's ear. Seeing my mom's eyes flicker as her sister spoke to her brought a rush of tears. One by one I called the rest of the relatives, who were all able to arrive by noon.

The family moved throughout the house, telling stories and individually saying their goodbyes. My cousin Thelma, seventy-five, sat next to Mom, brushing her soft brown hair with her hands. Loving touch is such an important gift to another. I watched my mother's eyes flutter and her pain dissipate each time someone held her hand.

Mom's breathing became shallower toward the afternoon. Edema turned her feet from pink to sky blue. My cousin Mark, so tall he hovered above me, anchored the room in stillness, and his physical presence provided support for me as we moved through the afternoon. The shallowness of my mother's breathing and the rippling sound of gurgles rising from her stomach were signs she would transition soon.

I found a Catholic priest, who before his five o'clock Mass, drove to my mother's home to perform last rites. As the family stood in a semicircle around the bed, he placed the sign of the cross over my mother's forehead. Her body twitched. She was aware of what was happening. I knew that she knew it was okay to let go. She also knew I was honoring her last wishes. The presence of love and light illuminated the den. I brushed my mother's hair with my hands. I whispered to her as I wiped the white foam coming from her nose. "It's okay, you can let go. There is nothing to worry about. Say hi to Aunt Lillian for me. Thank you for having me here with you. Thank you. I love you."

She squeezed my hand, acknowledging that she'd heard me. I left her bedside and went to sit in the garage, where Whitney Houston's "I Will Always Love You" played from the small radio in the corner. At 7:43 P.M. the door opened and my twenty-one-year-old niece said, "Uncle, Grandma's not breathing. Grandma's not breathing." A calmness came over me. I entered the house to find one young cousin crying on the floor of the laundry room and two other relatives crying around the kitchen table.

I walked slowly toward my mother. Her skin was clear, the edema gone, the wrinkles on her forehead gone, her body still warm, and her spirit moving through the room. A thick invisible fog lingered; it moved slowly. I stood over her body, surrounded by visible eyes watching for movement. I held her hand, still warm. Was she alive?

Kissing her forehead, I prayed in silence for Spirit to carry her to her next journey of life. Most family, friends, neighbors and the hospice team left by midnight. After the last car drove away, I returned to my mother's side. I perceived the presence of the energy of her spirit, although invisible and intangible, moving. With lights dimmed, I burned sage and prayed over my mother. I changed her clothing and washed her body. I brushed her hair and painted her lips. She was ready to go home.

# CHAPTER 12

# My Understanding Is Perfect

**December 18, 2011**

"Welcome to Business Class, Mr. Dobbins," exclaims the handsome Singaporean standing on the jet bridge. He marches me with a sway and a snap toward my seat. I am returning to Chicago in comfort. Green poinsettias and gold garlands are draped throughout the cabin, creating an ambiance that matches my slow monk-like movements. Once settled in my seat, I take a sip from a crystal flute filled with fresh orange juice and a squeeze of lime. As is my habit, I pull out my journal to unleash the fire moving inside me.

I make room for my inner child to speak. He shows me the spontaneous creativity flying through me. This feels like a holy moment. I savor the remembered sights, sounds and fragrances of the sea at Tanah Lot. I feel a peace, a love, a connection as I bask in the Divine presence. Internally I repeat my sacred word, visualizing the wonderment I experienced with a couple of breaths.

Then I sigh big long sighs, embracing my orphan-hood,

connecting to an inner silence, a stillness, a meditative state that leads me where Spirit meets soul. I recognize that I am on my own. I have experienced the healing of open wounds, which were stored in my luggage for unleashing.

My inner child showed me in Bali that I am a wizard juggling words and experiences, unscrambling magical sequences of intuitive synchronicity. He led the way in shaping my call to change, to uncoil the umbilical cord. He showed me how to move gracefully through the trauma and the hidden tears of formative wounds. He showed me the steps I must take to heal, to reclaim my life energy. He showed me the meaning of striving and unconscious limitations. He showed me a vision of my potential. He showed me through the words of a sacred chant:

> We come on this trek,
> To find our life,
> For we are all,
> We are all,
> We are all children of ...
>
> Brilliantly colored flower,
> A flaming flower.
> And there is no one,
> There is no one,
> Who regrets what we are.

Was she her own prisoner in that dark tunnel? Was she able to turn and walk toward the light without suffering pain from the glare? Did she enter a state of consciousness of joy, serenity, of clear understanding and radiant love? Is she in communion with Universal life? Did she embrace her imperfections and honor herself? Did she face the dark forces in her life, as she succumbed to the steel-plated hospital bed? Was she carried off on a creative high, transformed in her loving?

I was able to let go of the mask she placed over my eyes, and during our time together, see through the eyes of a child who had not known love, and through the eyes of the man whose inner child allowed him to recognize that he no longer had to please her at all costs. "What did I do wrong?" no longer caused him to doubt the significance of his existence.

She was neurotic at times, a shooting firecracker of irrationality, cocooned in her own unhappiness and fear. Did she ever understand the emptiness she felt inside? The light, the fire in her eyes, sizzled—a magnification of years of anger. Now closed, gone from the world— evaporated into nothingness.

She unknowingly provided me my initiation into life. She shaped my loss of innocence, she shaped my experience of disappointment, and she prepared me for my experience with betrayal and abandonment. But it was not until my feet were standing perfectly firm that I saw this story disappearing.

Did she feel the warmth of the daily glass mug in her hands, and feel the sacredness of the tea? Did she know love? Did her wrapped, washed, weightless body, now ash on earth, provide her with the power and energy for her transition?

A light enters me, showing me my child's sacrifice for love. I see that I was not forced to earn her love. I returned to care for her and I experienced a steady flow of grace and kindness. I relinquished the child she remembered and became the man who loved her, her son. Uncoiling in Bali, after 203 days, the frozen grief melted. I felt a positive thread woven to her spirit. I exposed myself, all of me, to the feelings, to my weakness. I accept my reality. I allow hurt, anger, pain, sadness to disperse. I am accountable for my choices. I choose to live without resentment. I stand knowing that I am not missing.

Transcendent in understanding, my ego dissolves as I merge with the great Oneness. I am renewed, grounded in the birth of new possibilities—connected to the Source of all life. I listen for the silence within, a warmth of silence.

# Acknowledgments

Gratitude and heartfelt appreciation for the support and kindness each of you has demonstrated as I embarked on the journey of writing *Tea with Mom*.

Mary T. Schneider, my sixth grade teacher from Emerson Elementary/Junior High in Oak Park, Illinois, whose guidance, words of encouragement and friendship has expanded every decade. I'm honored to have had a teacher whose impact and support I so deeply cherish.

My entrepreneur friend from San Francisco International Airport, Debbie Seanez, whose leadership has built a family dream.

Jamie Lee Silver, for your love and friendship; Olla McFern, for being a thread in my life from the beginning; Cheryl Stromstad-Synder, an angel on my journey; Randal Lucas for our intertwining fans of life; Cosmo Ferro for showing up and sharing your inner beauty; Henry Thompson, thank you for your laughter.

Chip Conley, thank you for bringing joy on my journey.

A special thank you to Claire Guinto, Craig Cassidy, Wanda Whitaker, Kathleen Wilcox-Reiss, Zach M. Javdan, Sharon Walsh Thompson, John Roven, Dianne Owens-Lewis, Tim Kreidler, Dr. Marcus Conant and my

Bali friend Stephen James Castley.

This book could not have come to a loving completion without the foundational love of Caterina A. Di Legge, Dr. Robert Fallat, Dr. Alison Lavoy and Dr. Pamela Noli.

A special thank you to Suzanne Potts and Darlene Frank, whose digital red ink spliced a tender weave and grace into my words and sentences on this incredible journey.

# About the Author

Eddie L. Dobbins, Jr. is a life coach, writer, realtor and modern elder entrepreneur. Through his coaching, healing work and global retreats, Eddie guides people to find the inner drive that helps bring their dreams to reality.

Eddie was born in the 1960's, into a segregated Chicago when public schools actively resisted integration. He recalls the Willis Wagons—aluminum trailers used as temporary schoolrooms to separate black children from white. At that time it was also illegal for his father, of African descent, and his mother, Caucasian, to marry.

Eddie's professional career includes building and leading teams in business development and sales in the hospitality and transportation industries. In 1999 he was a field strategist for the successful re-election of San Francisco Mayor Willie L. Brown, Jr.

After the campaign and a year spent writing in Italy, Eddie joined the San Francisco International Airport's Revenue Development Department, where he successfully created out-of-the-box revenue concepts and overhauled the airport food and beverage program to feature local restaurateurs.

Eddie then returned to the private sector as VP of

Channel Development for San Francisco startup Zoom, Inc., the global leader of automated retail. There he was responsible for brand management, directing channel teams, and developing strategic partnerships and initiatives. He worked closely with companies such as Best Buy, Apple and Sony.

In the winter of 2011, Eddie returned to Chicago to take on an unfamiliar role: that of caring for his dying mother. This experience, which became the subject of *Tea with Mom*, shifted their relationship. His love of Bali unfolded a gift of healing, where Eddie learned that in death, there is life.

Eddie earned an MA in Spiritual Psychology from the University of Santa Monica and a BA in Political Science from Simpson College in Iowa.

Visit Eddie's website at www.eddiedobbins.com.

CPSIA information can be obtained
at www.ICGtesting.com
Printed in the USA
FSHW021700240122
87877FS